LEAVES OF GRASS

LEAVES OF GRASS

THE FIRST EDITION 1855

WALT WHITMAN

EDITED, WITH AN INTRODUCTION BY

MALCOLM COWLEY

BARNES
&NOBLE
BOOKS
NEW YORK

Originally published as Walt Whitman's *Leaves of Grass, The First (1855) Edition*,
Edited, with an Introduction by Malcolm Cowley.

Introduction copyright © 1959 by The Viking Press, Inc.
Copyright renewed © 1987 by Malcolm Cowley.

This edition published by Barnes & Noble, Inc.,
by arrangement with Viking Penguin, a division
of Penguin Books USA, Inc.

1997 Barnes & Noble Books

ISBN 0-7607-0550-X

Printed and bound in the United States of America

02 03 04 05 M 12 11 10 9 8 7

RRDC

CONTENTS

[1] The poems had no titles in the first edition. The titles listed here, for the convenience of readers, are the ones that Whitman finally chose for them.

INTRODUCTION

THE FIRST EDITION of *Leaves of Grass,* as placed on sale July 4, 1855, bears little outside or inside resemblance to any of the later editions, which kept growing larger as Whitman added new poems. The original work is a thin folio about the size and shape of a block of typewriting paper. The binding is of dark-green pebbled cloth, and the title is stamped in gold, with the rustic letters sending down roots and sprouting above into leaves. Inside the binding are ninety-five printed pages, numbered iv–xii and 14–95. A prose introduction is set in double columns on the roman-numeraled pages, and the remaining text consists of twelve poems, as compared with 383 in the final or "Deathbed" edition. The first poem, later called "Song of Myself," is longer than the other eleven together. There is no table of contents, and none of the poems has a title.

Another calculated feature of the first edition is that the names of the author and the publisher—actually the same person—are omitted from the title page. Instead the opposite page contains a portrait: the engraved daguerreotype of a bearded man in his middle thirties, slouching under a wide-brimmed and high-crowned black felt hat that has "a rakish kind of slant," as the engraver said later, "like the mast of a schooner." His right hand is resting nonchalantly on his hip; the left is hidden in the pocket of his coarse-woven trousers. He wears no coat or waistcoat, and his shirt is thrown wide open at the collar to reveal a burly neck and the top of what seems to be a red-flannel undershirt. It is the portrait of a devil-may-care American working-man, one who might be taken as a somewhat idealized figure in almost any crowd.

His full name, though missing on the title page, appears twice in the first edition, but in different forms. On the copyright page we read, "*Entered according to Act of Congress in the year 1855, by* WALTER WHITMAN. . . ." On page 29, almost in the middle of the long first poem, we are introduced to "Walt Whitman, an American, one of the roughs, a kosmos." When a law-abiding citizen, even one of the roughs, changes his name even slightly, it is often because he wishes to assume a new personality. A reader might infer that *Walter* Whitman is the journeyman printer who had become a hack journalist, then a newspaper editor, before being lost to sight; whereas *Walt* Whitman is the workingman of the portrait and the putative author—but actual hero—of this extraordinary book.

No other book in the history of American letters was so completely an individual or do-it-yourself project. Not only did Whitman choose his idealized or dramatized self as subject of the book; not only did he create the new style in which it was written (working hard and intelligently to perfect the style over a period of six or seven years), but he also created the new personality of the proletarian bard who was supposed to have done the writing. When a manuscript of the poems was ready in the spring of 1855, Whitman's work was only beginning. He designed the book and arranged to have it printed at a job-printing shop in Brooklyn. He set some of the type himself, not without making errors. He did his best to get the book distributed, with the lukewarm cooperation of his friends the Fowler brothers, whose specialty was not bookselling but water cures and phrenology. He was his own press agent and even volunteered as critic of the book, writing three—or a majority—of the favorable reviews it received.

In spite of his best efforts not many copies were sold, and the first edition has never been widely read, except in the special world of literary scholars. The author himself might have been forgotten, if it had not been for a single fortunate event. One copy—not in pebbly green cloth, but paper bound—had been sent to Emerson, who was the most widely respected American of letters and the man best qualified to understand what the new poet was saying. Emerson wrote a letter of heartfelt thanks. When the letter was printed in the New York *Tribune*—without the writer's permission—it amazed and horrified the little American republic of letters. Nobody agreed with Emerson except a few of the extreme Transcendentalists, notably Thoreau and Alcott. Whitman was almost universally condemned, at least for the next ten years, but he would never again be merely a call in the midst of the crowd.

Concord   21 July
Masstts   1855

Dear Sir,

    I am not blind to the worth of the wonderful gift of "Leaves of Grass." I find it the most extraordinary piece of wit & wisdom that America has yet contributed. I am very happy in reading it, as great power makes us happy. It meets the demand I am always making of what seemed the sterile & stingy Nature, as if too much handiwork or too much lymph in the temperament were making our western wits fat & mean. I give you joy of your free & brave thought. I have great joy in it. I find incomparable things said incomparably well, as they must be. I find the courage of treatment, which so delights us, & which large perception only can inspire. I greet you at the beginning of a great career, which yet must have had a long foreground somewhere, for such a start. I rubbed my eyes a little to see if this sunbeam were no illusion; but the solid sense of the book is a sober certainty. It has the best merits, namely, of fortifying & encouraging.

    I did not know until I, last night, saw the book advertised in a newspaper, that I could trust the name as real & available for a post-office. I wish to see my benefactor, & have felt much like striking my tasks, & visiting New York to pay you my respects.

R. W. Emerson

Mr. Walter Whitman.

Emerson was being impulsive for a Concord man, but he was also trying to make his phrases accurate. Later, disapproving of Whitman's conduct, he would change his mind about the "great career." He would not and could not feel that most of the poems written after 1855 contained "incomparable things said incomparably well." But his praise of the first edition was unqualified, and it tempts me to make some unqualified statements of my own, as of simple truths that should have been recognized long ago.

First statement: that the long opening poem, later miscalled "Song of Myself," is Whitman's greatest work, perhaps his one completely realized work, and one of the great poems of modern times. Second, that the other eleven poems of the first edition are not on the same level of realization, but nevertheless are examples of Whitman's freshest and boldest style. At least four of them—their titles in the Deathbed edition are "To Think of Time," "The Sleepers," "I Sing the Body Electric," and "There Was a Child Went Forth"—belong in any selection of his best poems. Third, that the text of the first edition is the purest text for "Song of Myself," since many of the later corrections were also corruptions of the style and concealments of the original meaning. Fourth, that it is likewise the best text for most of the other eleven poems, but especially for "The Sleepers"—that fantasia of the unconscious—and "I Sing the Body Electric." And a final statement: that the first edition is a unified work, unlike any later edition, that it gives us a different picture of Whitman's achievement, and that—considering its very small circulation through the years—it might be called the buried masterpiece of American writing.

All that remains is to document some of these statements, not point by point, but chiefly in relation to "Song of Myself."

(2)

One reason among others why "Song of Myself" has been widely misprized and misinterpreted, especially by scholars, is that they have paid a disproportionate share of attention to its sources in contemporary culture. Besides noting many parallels with Emerson, they have found that it reflected a number of popular works and spectacles. Among these are Italian opera (notably as sung at the Astor Place Theatre in the great season of 1852–1853, when "Alboni's great self" paid her long and only visit to New York); George Sand's novel, *The Countess of Rudolstadt*, which presented the figure of a wandering bard and prophet (as well as another of her novels, *The Journeyman Joiner*, in which the hero was a carpenter and a proletarian saint); Frances Wright's then famous defense of Epicurean philosophy, *A Few Days in Athens*; the Count de Volney's *Ruins*, predicting the final union of all religions; Dr. Abbott's Egyptian Museum, on Broadway; O. M. Mitchel's book, *A Course of Six Lectures on Astronomy*, as well as other writings on the subject; and a number of essays clipped from the English quarterly reviews, of which the poet seems to have been a faithful reader. All these works and shows had a discernible influence on Whitman, but when they are listed with others and discussed at length they lead to one of the misconceptions that are the professional weakness of scholars. They tempt us to conclude that "Song of Myself" was merely a journalist's report, inspired but uneven, of popular culture in the 1850s. It was something more than that, and something vastly different from any of its literary sources.

I might suggest that the real nature of the poem becomes clearer when it is considered in relation to quite another list of works, even though Whitman had probably read none of them in 1855. Most of them he could not have read, because they were not yet written, or not published, or not translated into English. That other list might include the *Bhagavad-Gita*, the *Upanishads*, Christopher Smart's long crazy inspired poem *Jubilate Agno*, Blake's prophetic books (not forgetting *The Marriage of Heaven and Hell*), Rimbaud's *Illuminations*, *The Chants of Maldoror*, and Nietzsche's *Thus Spake Zarathustra*, as well as *The Gospel of Sri Ramakrishna* and a compendious handbook, *The Philosophies of India*, by Heinrich Zimmer (New York, 1951). I am offering what might seem to be a curious list of titles, but its double purpose is easy to explain. "Song of Myself" should be judged, I think, as one of the great inspired (and sometimes insane) prophetic works that have appeared at intervals in the Western world, like *Jubilate Agno* (which is written in a biblical style sometimes suggesting Whitman's), like the *Illuminations*, like *Thus Spake Zarathustra*. But the system of doctrine suggested by the poem is more Eastern than Western, it includes notions like metempsychosis and karma, and it might almost be one of those *Philosophies of India* that Zimmer expounds at length.

What is extraordinary about this Eastern element is that Whitman, when he was writing the poems of the first edition, seems to have known little or nothing about Indian philosophy. It is more than doubtful that he had even read the *Bhagavad-Gita,* one of the few Indian works then available in translation. He does not refer to it in his notebooks of the early 1850s, where he mentions most of the books he was poring over. A year after the first edition was published, Thoreau went to see him in Brooklyn and told him that *Leaves of Grass* was "Wonderfully like the Orientals." Had Whitman read them? he asked. The poet answered, "No: tell me about them." He seems to have taken advantage of Thoreau's reading list, since words from the Sanskrit (notably "Maya" and "sudra") are used correctly in some of the poems written after 1858. They do not appear in "Song of Myself," in spite of the recognizably Indian ideas expressed in the poem, and I would hazard the guess that the ideas are not of literary derivation. It is true that they were vaguely in the air of the time and that Whitman may have breathed them in from the Transcendentalists or even from some of the English quarterly reviewers. It also seems possible, however, that he reinvented them for himself, after an experience similar to the one for which the Sanskrit word is samadhi, or absorption.

What it must have been was a mystical experience in the proper sense of the term. Dr. Richard Maurice Bucke, the most acute of Whitman's immediate disciples, believed that it took place on a June morning in 1853 or 1854. He also believed that it was repeated on other occasions, but neither these nor the original experience can be dated from Whitman's papers. On the other hand, his notebooks and manuscripts of the early 1850s are full of sidelong references to such an experience, and they suggest that it was essentially the same as the illuminations or ecstasies of earlier bards and prophets. Such ecstasies consist in a rapt feeling of union or identity with God (or the Soul, or Mankind, or the Cosmos), a sense of ineffable joy leading to the conviction that the seer has been released from the limitations of space and time and has been granted a direct vision of truths impossible to express. As Whitman says in the famous fifth chant of "Song of Myself":

> Swiftly arose and spread around me the peace and joy and
>   knowledge that pass all the art and argument of the earth;
> And I know that the hand of God is the elderhand of my own,
> And I know that the spirit of God is the eldest brother of my own,
> And that all the men ever born are also my brothers . . . and the
>   women my sisters and lovers.

It is to be noted that there is no argument about the real occurrence of such ecstasies. They have been reported, sometimes in sharp detail, by men and women of many different nations, at many historical periods, and each report seems to bear a family resemblance to the others. Part of the resemblance is a feeling universally expressed by mystics that they have acquired a special sort of knowledge not learned from others, but directly revealed to the inner eye. This supposed knowledge has given independent rise to many systems of philosophy or cosmology, once again in many different cultures, and once again there is or should be no argument about one feature of almost all the systems or bodies of teaching: that they too have a family resemblance, like the experiences on which they are based. Indeed, they hold so many principles in common that it is possible for Aldous Huxley and others to group them all together as "the perennial philosophy."

The arguments, which will never end, are first about the nature of the mystical state—is it a form of self-hypnosis, is it a pathological condition to be induced by fasting, vigils, drugs, and other means of abusing the physical organism, or is it, as Whitman believed, the result of superabundant health and energy?—and then about the source and value of the philosophical notions to which it gives rise. Do these merely express the unconscious desires of the individual, and chiefly his sexual desires? Or, as Jungian psychologists like to suggest, are they derived from a racial or universally human unconscious? Are they revelations or hallucinations? Are they supreme doctrines, or are they heretical, false, and even satanic? They belong in the orthodox tradition of Indian philosophy. In Western Christianity, as also in Mohammedanism, the pure and self-consistent forms of mysticism are usually regarded as heresies, with the result that several of the medieval mystics were burned at the stake (though Theresa of Avila and John of the Cross found an orthodox interpretation for their visions and became saints).

Whitman cannot be called a Christian heretic, for the simple reason that he was not a Christian at any stage of his career, early or late. In some of the poems written after the Civil War, and in revisions of older poems made at the same time, he approached the Christian notion of a personal God, whom he invoked as the Elder Brother or the great Camerado. But then he insisted—in another poem of the same period, "Chanting the Square Deific"—that God was not a trinity but a quaternity, and that one of his faces was the "sudra face" of Satan. In "Song of Myself" as originally written, God is neither a person nor, in the strict sense, even a being; God is an abstract principle of energy that is manifested in every living creature, as well as in "the grass that grows wherever the land is and the water is." In some ways this God of the first edition resembles Emerson's Oversoul, but he seems much closer to the Brahman of the *Upanishads*, the absolute, unchanging, all-enfolding Consciousness, the Divine Ground from which all things emanate and to which all living things may hope to return. And this Divine Ground is by no means the only conception that Whitman shared with Indian philosophers, in the days when he was writing "Song of Myself."

(3)

The poem is hardly at all concerned with American nationalism, political democracy, contemporary progress, or other social themes that are commonly associated with Whitman's work. The "incomparable things" that Emerson found in it are philosophical and religious principles. Its subject is a state of illumination induced by two (or three) separate moments of ecstasy. In more or less narrative sequence it describes those moments, their sequels in life, and the doctrines to which they give rise. The doctrines are not expounded by logical steps or supported by arguments; instead they are presented dramatically, that is, as the new convictions of a hero, and they are revealed by successive unfoldings of his states of mind.

The hero as pictured in the frontispiece—this hero named "I" or "Walt Whitman" in the text—should not be confused with the Whitman of daily life. He is, as I said, a dramatized or idealized figure, and he is put forward as a representative American workingman, but one who prefers to loaf and invite his soul. Thus, he is rough, sunburned, bearded; he cocks his hat as he pleases, indoors or out; but in the text of the first edition he has no local or family background, and he is deprived of strictly individual characteristics, with the exception of curiosity, boastfulness, and an abnormally developed sense of touch. His really distinguishing feature is that he has been granted a vision, as a result of which he has realized the potentialities latent in every American and indeed, he says, in every living person, even "the brutish koboo, called the ordure of humanity." This dramatization of the hero makes it possible for the living Whitman to exalt him—as he would not have ventured, at the time, to exalt himself—but also to poke mild fun at the hero for his gab and loitering, for his tall talk or "omnivorous words," and for sounding his barbaric yawp over the roofs of the world. The religious feeling in "Song of Myself" is counterpoised by a humor that takes the form of slangy and mischievous impudence or drawling Yankee self-ridicule.

There has been a good deal of discussion about the structure of the poem. In spite of revealing analyses made by a few Whitman scholars, notably Carl F. Strauch and James E. Miller, Jr., a feeling still seems to prevail that it has no structure properly speaking; that it is inspired but uneven, repetitive, and especially weak in its transitions from one theme to another. I suspect that much of this feeling may be due to Whitman's later changes in the text, including his arbitrary scheme, first introduced in the 1867 edition, of dividing the poem into fifty-two numbered paragraphs or chants. One is tempted to read the chants as if they were separate poems, thus overlooking the unity and flow of the work as a whole. It may also be, however, that most of the scholars have been looking for a geometrical pattern, such as can be found and diagramed in some of the later poems. If there is no such pattern in "Song of Myself," that is because the poem was written on a different principle, one much closer to the spirit of the Symbolists or even the Surrealists.

The true structure of the poem is not primarily logical but psychological, and is not a geometrical figure but a musical progression. As music "Song of Myself" is not a symphony with contrasting movements, nor is it an operatic work like "Out of the Cradle Endlessly Rocking," with an overture, arias, recitatives, and a finale. It comes closer to being a rhapsody or tone poem, one that modulates from theme to theme, often changing in key and tempo, falling into reveries and rising toward moments of climax, but always preserving its unity of feeling as it moves onward in a wavelike flow. It is a poem that bears the marks of having been conceived as a whole and written in one prolonged burst of inspiration, but its unity is also the result of conscious art, as can be seen from Whitman's corrections in the early manuscripts. He did not recognize all the bad lines, some of which survive in the printed text, but there is no line in the first edition that seems false to a single prevailing tone. There are passages weaker than others, but none without a place in the general scheme. The repetitions are always musical variations and amplifications. Some of the transitions seem abrupt when the poem is read as if it were an essay, but Whitman was not working in terms of "therefore" and "however." He preferred to let one image suggest another image, which in turn suggests a new statement of mood or doctrine. His themes modulate into one another by pure association, as in a waking dream, with the result that all his transitions seem instinctively right.

In spite of these oneiric elements, the form of the poem is something more than a forward movement in rising and subsiding waves of emotion. There is also a firm narrative structure, one that becomes easier to grasp when we start by dividing the poem into a number of parts or sequences. I think there are nine of these, but the exact number is not important; another critic might say there were seven (as Professor Miller does), or eight or ten. Some of the transitions are gradual, and in such cases it is hard to determine the exact line that ends one sequence and starts another. The essential point is that the parts, however defined, follow one another in irreversible order, like the beginning, middle, and end of any good narrative. My own outline, not necessarily final, would run as follows:

First sequence (chants 1–4): the poet or hero introduced to his audience. Leaning and loafing at his ease, "observing a spear of summer grass," he presents himself as a man who lives outdoors and worships his own naked body, not the least part of which is vile. He is also in love with his deeper self or soul, but explains that it is not to be confused with his mere personality. His joyful contentment can be shared by you, the listener, "For every atom belonging to me as good belongs to you."

Second sequence (chant 5): the ecstasy. This consists in the rapt union of the poet and his soul, and it is described—figuratively, on the present occasion—in terms of sexual union. The poet now has a sense of loving brotherhood with God and with all mankind. His eyes being truly open for the first time, he sees that even the humblest objects contain the infinite universe—

And limitless are leaves stiff or drooping in the fields,
And brown ants in little wells beneath them,
And mossy scabs of the wormfence, and heaped stones, and elder
    and mullen and pokeweed.

Third sequence (chants 6–19): the grass. Chant 6 starts with one of Whitman's brilliant transitions. A child comes with both hands full of those same leaves from the fields. "What is the grass?" the child asks—and suddenly we are presented with the central image of the poem, that is, the grass as symbolizing the miracle of common things and the divinity (which implies both the equality and the immortality) of ordinary persons. During the remainder of the sequence, the poet observes men and women—and animals too—at their daily occupations. He is part of this life, he says, and even his thoughts are those of all men in all ages and lands. There are two things to be noted about the sequence, which contains some of Whitman's freshest lyrics. First, the people with a few exceptions (such as the trapper and his bride) are those whom Whitman has known all his life, while the scenes described at length are Manhattan streets and Long Island beaches or countryside. Second, the poet merely roams, watches, and listens, like a sort of Tiresias. The keynote of the sequence—as Professor Strauch was the first to explain—is the two words "I observe."

Fourth sequence (chants 20–25): the poet in person. "Hankering, gross, mystical, nude," he venerates himself as august and immortal, but so, he says, is everyone else. He is the poet of the body and of the soul, of night, earth, and sea, and of vice and feebleness as well as virtue, so that "many long dumb voices" speak through his lips, including those of slaves, prostitutes, even beetles rolling balls of dung. All life to him is such a miracle of beauty that the sunrise would kill him if he could not find expression for it—"If I could not now and always send sunrise out of me." The sequence ends with a dialogue between the poet and his power of speech, during which the poet insists that his deeper self—"the best I am"—is beyond expression.

Fifth sequence (chants 26–29): ecstasy through the senses. Beginning with chant 26, the poem sets out in a new direction. The poet decides to be completely passive: "I think I will do nothing for a long time but listen." What he hears at first are quiet familiar sounds like the gossip of flames on the hearth and the bustle of growing wheat; but the sounds rise quickly to a higher pitch, becoming the matchless voice of a trained soprano, and he is plunged into an ecstasy of hearing, or rather of Being. Then he starts over again, still passively, with the sense of touch, and finds himself rising to the ecstasy of sexual union. This time the union is actual, not figurative, as can be seen from the much longer version of chant 29 preserved in an early notebook.

Sixth sequence (chants 30–38): the power of identification. After his first ecstasy, as presented in chant 5, the poet had acquired a sort of microscopic vision that enabled him to find infinite wonders in the smallest and most familiar things. The second ecstasy (or pair of ecstasies) has an entirely different effect, conferring as it does a sort of vision that is both telescopic and spiritual. The poet sees far into space and time; "afoot with my vision" he ranges over the continent and goes speeding through the heavens among tailed meteors. His secret is the power of identification. Since everything emanates from the universal soul, and since his own soul is of the same essence, he can identify himself with every object and with every person living or dead, heroic or criminal. Thus, he is massacred with the Texans at Goliad, he fights on the *Bonhomme Richard*, he dies on the cross, and he rises again as "one of an average unending procession." Whereas the keynote of the third sequence was "I observe," here it becomes "I am"—"I am a free companion"—"My voice is the wife's voice, the screech by the rail of the stairs"—"I am the man. . . . I suffered. . . . I was there."

Seventh sequence (chants 39–41): the superman. When Indian sages emerge from the state of samadhi or absorption, they often have the feeling of being omnipotent. It is so with the poet, who now feels gifted with superhuman powers. He is the universally beloved Answerer (chant 39), then the Healer, raising men from their deathbeds (40), and then the Prophet (41) of a new religion that outbids "the old cautious hucksters" by announcing that men are divine and will eventually be gods.

Eighth sequence (chants 42–50): the sermon. "A call in the midst of the crowd" is the poet's voice, "orotund sweeping and final." He is about to offer a statement of the doctrines implied by the narrative (but note that his statement comes at the right point psychologically and plays its part in the narrative sequence). As strangers listen, he proclaims that society is full of injustice, but that the reality beneath it is deathless persons (chant 42); that he accepts and practices all religions, but looks beyond them to "what is untried and afterward"

(43); that he and his listeners are the fruit of ages, and the seed of untold ages to be (44); that our final goal is appointed: "God will be there and wait till we come" (45); that he tramps a perpetual journey and longs for companions, to whom he will reveal a new world by washing the gum from their eyes—but each must then continue the journey alone (46); that he is the teacher of men who work in the open air (47); that he is not curious about God, but sees God everywhere, at every moment (48); that we shall all be reborn in different forms ("No doubt I have died myself ten thousand times before"); and that the evil in the world is like moonlight, a mere reflection of the sun (49). The end of the sermon (chant 50) is the hardest passage to interpret in the whole poem. I think, though I cannot be certain, that the poet is harking back to the period after one of his ten thousand deaths, when he slept and slept long before his next awakening. He seems to remember vague shapes, and he beseeches these Outlines, as he calls them, to let him reveal the "word unsaid." Then turning back to his audience, "It is not chaos or death," he says. "It is form and union and plan. . . . it is eternal life. . . . it is happiness."

Ninth sequence (chants 51–52) : the poet's farewell. Having finished his sermon, the poet gets ready to depart, that is, to die and wait for another incarnation or "fold of the future," while still inviting others to follow. At the beginning of the poem he had been leaning and loafing at ease in the summer grass. Now, having rounded the circle, he bequeaths himself to the dirt "to grow from the grass I love." I do not see how any careful reader, unless blinded with preconceptions, could overlook the unity of the poem in tone and image and direction.

(4)

It is in the eighth sequence, which is a sermon, that Whitman gives us most of the doctrines suggested by his mystical experience, but they are also implied in the rest of the poem and indeed in the whole text of the first edition. Almost always he expresses them in the figurative and paradoxical language that prophets have used from the beginning.

Now I should like to state them explicitly, even at the cost of some repetition.

Whitman believed when he was writing "Song of Myself"—and at later periods too, but with many changes in emphasis—that there is a distinction between one's mere personality and the deeper Self (or between ego and soul). He believed that the Self (or atman, to use a Sanskrit word) is of the same essence as the universal spirit (though he did not quite say it *is* the universal spirit, as Indian philosophers do in the phrase "Atman is Brahman"). He believed that true knowledge is to be acquired not through the senses or the intellect, but through union with the Self. At such moments of union (or "merge," as Whitman called it) the gum is washed from one's eyes (that is his own phrase), and one can read an infinite lesson in common things, discovering that a mouse, for example, "is miracle enough to stagger sextillions of infidels." This true knowledge is available to every man and woman, since each conceals a divine Self. Moreover, the divinity of all implies the perfect equality of all, the immortality of all, and the universal duty of loving one another.

Immortality for Whitman took the form of metempsychosis, and he believed that every individual will be reborn, usually but not always in a higher form. He had also worked out for himself something approaching the Indian notion of karma, which is the doctrine that actions performed during one incarnation determine the nature and fate of the individual during his next incarnation; the doctrine is emphatically if somewhat unclearly stated in a passage of his prose introduction that was later rewritten as a poem, "Song of Prudence." By means of metempsychosis and karma, we are all involved in a process of spiritual evolution that might be compared to natural evolution. Even the latter process, however, was not regarded by Whitman as strictly natural or material. He believed that animals have a rudimentary sort of soul ("They bring me tokens of myself"), and he hinted or surmised, without directly saying, that rocks, trees, and planets possess an identity, or "eidólon," that persists as they rise to higher states of being. The double process of evolution, natural and spiritual, can be traced for ages into the past, and he believed that it will continue for ages beyond ages. Still, it is not an eternal process, since it has an ultimate goal, which appears to be the reabsorption of all things into the Divine Ground.

Most of Whitman's doctrines, though by no means all of them, belong to the mainstream of Indian philosophy. In some respects he went against the stream. Unlike most of the Indian sages, for example, he was not a thoroughgoing idealist. He did not believe that the whole world of the senses, of desires, of birth and death, was only maya, illusion, nor did he hold that it was a sort of purgatory; instead he praised the world as real and joyful. He did not despise the body, but proclaimed that it was as miraculous as the soul. He was too good a citizen of the nineteenth century to surrender his faith in material progress as the necessary counterpart of spiritual progress. Although he yearned for ecstatic union with the soul or Oversoul, he did not try to achieve it by subjugating the senses, as advised by yogis and Buddhists alike; on the contrary, he thought the "merge" could also be achieved (as in chants 26–29) by a total surrender to the senses. These are important differences, but it must be remembered that Indian philosophy or theology is not such a unified structure as it appears to us from a distance. Whitman might have found Indian sages or gurus and even whole sects that agreed with one or another of his heterodoxies (perhaps excepting his belief in material progress). One is tempted to say that instead of being a Christian heretic, he was an Indian rebel and sectarian.

Sometimes he seems to be a Mahayana Buddhist, promising nirvana for all after countless reincarnations, and also sharing the belief of some Mahayana sects that the sexual act can serve as one of the sacraments. At other times he might be an older brother of Sri Ramakrishna (1836–1886), the nineteenth-century apostle of Tantric Brahmanism and of joyous affirmation. Although this priest of Kali, the Mother Goddess, refused to learn English, one finds him delivering some of Whitman's messages in—what is more surprising—the same tone of voice. Read, for example, this fairly typical passage from *The Gospel of Sri Ramakrishna,* while remembering that "Consciousness" is to be taken here as a synonym for Divinity:

> The Divine Mother revealed to me in the Kali temple that it was She who had become everything. She showed me that everything was full of Consciousness. The Image was Consciousness, the altar was Consciousness, the water-vessels were Consciousness, the door-sill was Consciousness, the marble floor was Consciousness —all was Consciousness. . . . I saw a wicked man in front of the Kali temple; but in him I saw the Power of the Divine Mother vibrating. That was why I fed a cat with the food that was to be offered to the Divine Mother.

Whitman expresses the same idea at the end of chant 48, and in the same half-playful fashion:

Why should I wish to see God better than this day?
I see something of God each hour of the twenty-four, and each
   moment then,
In the faces of men and women I see God, and in my own face in
   the glass;
I find letters from God dropped in the street, and every one is
   signed by God's name,
And I leave them where they are, for I know that others will
   punctually come forever and ever.

Such parallels—and there are dozens that might be quoted—are more than accidental. They reveal a kinship in thinking and experience that can be of practical value to students of Whitman. Since the Indian mystical philosophies are elaborate structures, based on conceptions that have been shaped and defined by centuries of discussion, they help to explain Whitman's ideas at points in the first edition where he seems at first glance to be vague or self-contradictory. There is, for example, his unusual combination of realism—sometimes brutal realism—and serene optimism. Today he is usually praised for the first, blamed for the second (optimism being out of fashion), and blamed still more for the inconsistency he showed in denying the existence of evil. The usual jibe is that Whitman thought the universe was perfect and was getting better every day.

It is obvious, however, that he never meant to deny the existence of evil in himself or his era or his nation. He knew that it existed in his own family, where one of his brothers was a congenital idiot, another was a drunkard married to a streetwalker, and still another, who had caught "the bad disorder," later died of general paresis in an insane asylum. Whitman's doctrine implied that each of them would have an opportunity to avoid those misfortunes or punishments in another incarnation, where each would be rewarded for his good actions. The universe was an eternal becoming for Whitman, a process not a structure, and it had to be judged from the standpoint of eternity. After his mystical experience, which seemed to offer a vision of eternity, he had become convinced that evil existed only as part of a universally perfect design. That explains his combination of realism and optimism, which seems unusual only in our Western world. In India, Heinrich Zimmer says, "Philosophic theory, religious belief, and intuitive experience support each other . . . in the basic insight that, fundamentally, all is well. A supreme optimism prevails everywhere, in spite of the unromantic recognition that the universe of man's affairs is in the most imperfect state imaginable, one amounting practically to chaos."

Another point explained by Indian conceptions is the sort of democracy Whitman was preaching in "Song of Myself." There is no doubt that he was always a democrat politically—which is to say a Jacksonian Democrat, a Barnburner writing editorials against the Hunkers, a Free Soiler in sympathy, and then a liberal but not a radical Republican. He remained faithful to what he called "the good old cause" of liberty, equality, and fraternity, and he wrote two moving elegies for the European rebels of 1848. In "Song of Myself," however, he is not advocating rebellion or even reform. "To a drudge of the cottonfields," he says, "or emptier of privies I lean. . . . on his right cheek I put the family kiss"; but he offers nothing more than a kiss and an implied promise. What he preaches throughout the poem is not political but religious democracy, such as was practiced by the early Christians. Today it is practiced, at least in theory, by the Tantric sect, and we read in *Philosophies of India*:

> All beings and things are members of a single mystic family (*kula*). There is therefore no thought of caste within the Tantric holy "circles" (*cakra*). . . . Women as well as men are eligible not only to receive the highest initiation but also to confer it in the role of guru. . . . However, it must not be supposed that this indifference to the rules of caste implies any idea of revolution within the social sphere, as distinguished from the sphere of spiritual progress. The initiate returns to his post in society; for there too is the manifestation of Sakti. The world is affirmed, just as it is—neither renounced, as by an ascetic, nor corrected, as by a social reformer.

The promise that Whitman offers to the drudge of the cottonfields, the emptier of privies, and the prostitute draggling her shawl is that they too can set out with him on his perpetual journey—perhaps not in their present incarnations, but at least in some future life. And that leads to another footnote offered by the Indian philosophies: they explain what the poet meant by the Open Road. It starts as an actual road that winds through fields and cities, but Whitman is doing more than inviting us to shoulder our duds and go hiking along it. The real journey is toward spiritual vision, toward reunion with the Divine Ground; and thus the Open Road becomes Whitman's equivalent for all the other roads and paths and ways that appear in mystical teachings. It reminds us of the Noble Eightfold Path of the Buddhists, and the Taoist Way; it suggests both the *bhakti-marga* or "path of devotion" and the *karma-marga* or "path of sacrifice"; while it comes closer to being the "big ferry" of the Mahayana sect, in which there is room for every soul to cross to the farther shore. Whitman's conception, however, was even broader. He said one should know "the universe itself as a road, as many roads, as roads for traveling souls."

I am not pleading for the acceptance of Whitman's ideas or for any other form of mysticism, Eastern or Western. I am only suggesting that his ideas as expressed in "Song of Myself" were bolder and more coherent than is generally supposed, and philosophically a great deal more respectable.

(5)

But there is more to be said in judgment of Whitman and his work. It was a truly extraordinary achievement for him to rediscover the outlines of a whole philosophical system chiefly on the basis of his own mystical experience and with little help from his reading. Frances Wright's *A Few Days in Athens*? Volney's *Ruins*? *De Rerum Natura*? The novels of George Sand? There is hardly a hint of them in Whitman's fundamental thinking, although there is more than a hint of Emerson's Neoplatonism. But Emerson, who regarded himself as a teacher not a prophet, had nothing to do with notions like metempsychosis or karma or the universe pictured as a road for traveling souls. His temporary disciple felt that he had gone far beyond the teacher and was venturing into an unexplored continent of the Self. What does it matter that his sense of discovery was largely based on ignorance of the mystical tradition! It could still encourage him to make real discoveries in style and symbol, and it could arouse a feeling of release and exhilaration in his readers.

This aspect of "Song of Myself" becomes clearer when the poem is compared with another long work about the mystical experience, T. S. Eliot's *Four Quartets*. The works have more in common than Eliot has realized, but there is a fundamental difference that leads to many others. Eliot could never have made the mistake of thinking that his experience was the first of its kind. He knows the tradition thoroughly and can always dignify his personal memories with quotations or half-quotations from the *Bhagavad-Gita* (which he read long ago in Sanskrit), from John of the Cross, *The Cloud of Unknowing*, and the anchoret Juliana of Norwich. Using craftsmanship as well as learning, he has invented a rich structure for *Four Quartets*, so that it becomes a magnificent exercise in architectonics. What we miss in the poem may be simply the exhilaration that comes from a sense of discovery. Even in his mystical experience, Eliot cannot forget the lesson of caution he has learned from his studies. He knows that his eternal moment in the rose garden will last for a moment only. He knows that he must go back to his usual state of being, and then—

> Ridiculous the waste sad time
> Stretching before and after.

Disciplined as he is by tradition, Eliot makes few mistakes of any sort; nor does he encourage his disciples to make them (except sometimes the great mistake of shrinking into dryness and pedantry). Whitman, on the other hand, misleads as much as he inspires, and there is no doubt that he has had a fatal influence on some of his disciples. There is also no doubt that he was the first to be misled, and very soon after writing "Song of Myself." At that point his exhilarating pride of discovery began to change into humorless arrogance. If he had been as familiar with the mystical tradition as Eliot shows himself to be, Whitman would have been warned against the feeling of omnipotence that, as we have seen, often follows a mystical experience. We read in *Philosophies of India* that the adept reaches a point in his spiritual progress at which he becomes identified with the personal creator of the world illusion. "He feels," Dr. Zimmer continues, "that he is at one with the Supreme Lord, partaking of His virtues of omniscience and omnipotence. This, however, is a dangerous phase; for if he is to go to Brahman, the goal, he must realize that this inflation is only a subtle form of self-delusion. The candidate must conquer it, press beyond it, so that the anonymity of sheer being (*sat*), consciousness (*cit*), and bliss (*ananda*) may break upon him as the transpersonal essence of his actual Self."

Whitman, of course, had never heard of this purely anonymous or transpersonal state. Remaining for a long time in the dangerous phase of self-inflation (or "dilation," as he called it) and regarding himself as a God-inspired prophet, he kept looking about for other new doctrines to prophesy. The first of these he found was a rather bumptious American nationalism, which is already suggested in his prose introduction to the first edition of *Leaves of Grass* (written after the poems), but which becomes more explicit in the new poems of the second or 1856 edition. Also in the second edition, he announced himself in an open letter to Emerson ("Dear Master") as the prophet of unashamed sex. In 1857 he determined to become what he called a "wander speaker"—"perhaps launching at the President, leading persons, Congressmen or Judges of the Supreme Court . . . the greatest champion America ever could know, yet holding no office or emolument whatever—but first in the esteem of men and women." Soon afterward he dreamed of founding a new religion, for which *Leaves of Grass*—expanded into 365 chapters or psalms, one to be read on each day of the year—would serve as a holy testament. Preserved among his papers is a note to himself that reads: "The Great Construction of the New Bible. Not to be diverted from the principal object—the main life work—the three hundred and sixty-five. It ought to be ready in 1859." During those years before the Civil War, Whitman was afflicted with megalomania to such an extent that he was losing touch with the realities, or at least the human possibilities, of American life.

At the same time he was making—if judged by the mystical tradition—another blunder against which the Indians might have warned him. He had once been careful to distinguish the external self or personality from the deeper Self that he was celebrating in his greatest poem. Now he forgot the distinction and began to celebrate "myself" in the guise of a simple separate person—greater than other persons, no longer standing aloof and unperturbed, but greedy for praise and tortured with desires. This person, however, laid claim to all the liberties and powers that Whitman had once ascribed to the transpersonal Self. Anything that the person felt like saying was also the right and inspired thing to say. Composing great poems was a simple matter. All the person had to do was permit Nature—*his* nature—to speak "without check with original energy."

While dreaming his crazy dreams, Whitman continued to live with his family in a little frame workingman's house in Brooklyn, where he shared a bed with his idiot brother. Thoreau on his first visit noted that the bed was unmade and that an unemptied chamber-pot stood beneath it. Other literary men described their meetings with Whitman in a tone of fascinated horror that suggests the accounts of present-day visitors to North Beach or Big Sur or Venice West. Indeed, one cannot help feeling that the Whitman of those days was a predecessor of the beatniks: he had the beard, the untrimmed hair, and although his costume was different, it might be regarded as the 1860 equivalent of sweatshirt and sandals. Some of his conduct also resembled that of the Beat Generation. He stayed out of the rat race, he avoided the squares (preferring the company of omnibus drivers and deck hands on the ferries); he was "real gone," he was "far out"; and he was writing poems in what Lawrence Lipton calls "the 'open,' free-swinging style that is prized in Beat Generation literature." Some of them should be read to loud music as a means of glossing over their faults and holding the listener's attention—not to the music of a jazz combo, like beatnik poetry, but perhaps to that of a regimental brass band.

A poet's conduct and his work are two ways of expressing the same habits of thinking. It was during those years just before the Civil War that Whitman first indulged himself in a whole collection of stylistic mannerisms. He had once planned to write in what he called "A perfectly transparent, plate-glassy style, artless, with no ornaments, or attempts at ornaments, for their own sake." He had planned to use "Common idioms and phrases—Yankeeisms and vulgarisms—cant expressions when very pat only." The effect he wanted to achieve was one of "Clearness, simplicity, no twistified or foggy sentences, at all—the most translucid clearness without variations"; and that was one of the effects he did achieve in the first edition, except in a few gangling passages and a few others where he was being deliberately hermetic. It was after 1855 that he began to cultivate his bad habits of speech—such, for example, as unnecessary or "poetic" inversions; as foreign words, often used incorrectly and without good reason (there had been only a few of them in "Song of Myself"); as ugly new words of his own coinage; as the "I" placed obtrusively at the end of a phrase

("No dainty dolce affettuoso I"); as the Quaker names for months and days, such as "Fourth-month" for April and "First-day" for Sunday (which might have been excusable if Whitman had been a Quaker); and as, worst of all, the interminable bald inventories that read like the names of parts and organs in an anatomical chart or like the index to a school geography. In the first edition he had broken most of the nineteenth-century rules for elegant writing, but now he was violating an older literary convention, that of simply being considerate of one's readers.

Whitman's beatnik period, however, proved to be only a transitory phase of a life that had several other phases. The best record of his attitude during the period is the greatly expanded text of the third or 1860 edition, which is an engaging and impressive book for all its extravagant gestures, and which, after the first, is the other vintage edition of his poems. Soon after it was published, the Civil War gave a new direction to Whitman's career. His war poems are disappointing, with two or three exceptions, but his unselfish service in army hospitals helped to establish him in still another personality, one he kept to the end: that of the good gray poet, and it was during the post-war years that he produced some of his most important work. Much of it shows that he was turning back toward the Eastern beliefs expressed in "Song of Myself." Perhaps the return was caused by another mystical experience, but although the supposition seems a likely one, the only evidence to support it consists of scattered passages in his two prose works of the time, *Democratic Vistas* and *Specimen Days*. We know, however, that he planned at the time to make "Passage to India" the title not merely of a long poem about the journey of the soul toward God, but of a whole volume "bridging the way," as he said, "from life to death."

The volume would be designed to stand beside *Leaves of Grass*, which he had come to regard as a finished work. Some of the poems he planned to put into the new book—"Proud Music of the Storm," "Prayer of Columbus," and most of all "Passage to India" itself—are truly admirable in conception and in their rich symphonic structure. The language, however, is more abstract and a great deal less vivid or Yankee than that of the first edition (besides retaining most of the mannerisms developed in his period of self-inflation). If he did have another mystical experience before writing the poems, it failed to give him the miraculously fresh vision of familiar people and objects that had followed his earlier illumination. As for the creed put forward in "Passage to India" and other poems of the same period, it is no longer purely mystical, being mixed with the ambiguous doctrine of male comradeship or "adhesiveness" that Whitman had first expressed in the "Calamus" poems of the 1860 edition, and mixed again with his still more recent doctrine of Personalism. The deeper Self is now identified with the personality (or eidólon, as he was beginning to call it). God Himself becomes personal (or four-personal, in "Chanting the Square Deific") and is addressed as the Older Brother of the soul.

Soon the notion of publishing a grand new book had to be put aside, as a result of the apoplectic stroke that Whitman suffered in January 1873. He lived nineteen years longer and wrote scores of poems, but most of them were occasional verses bearing a curious resemblance to his newspaper editorials of the 1840s. The only ambitious work he finished was "Dream of Columbus" (1874), which served as a dignified and moving peroration to his career. He retired to Camden, New Jersey, where he lived serenely and received a good many visitors, most of them his devoted followers, so that he presented the picture of an Indian guru surrounded by his *adhikarin* or disciples.

During the first years in Camden Whitman spent a good deal of time revising his early poems, in the hope of reshaping his extremely diversified work into an organic whole. Most of the revisions were designed to make his style more uniform, to bring his teaching up to date, or to gloss over the differences between what he had once said and what he now believed. "Do I contradict myself?" Once Whitman had asked the question defiantly, but now it worried him. He still regarded himself as a prophet, and a prophet's duty is to have been always right. It would have been better for his strictly poetic reputation if he had allowed the early illuminated Whitman to speak for himself, the bohemian or inflated Whitman to speak for himself, and the good gray poet to speak for himself, each in his separate fashion.

(6)

In the collection of variorum readings compiled long ago by Oscar Lovell Triggs, the revisions in "Song of Myself" occupy thirty pages. Triggs found that Whitman had changed the wording of all but five of the fifty-two chants into which he had finally divided the poem. In those five—chants 9, 27, 28, 29, and 52—the only changes are in punctuation and spelling. Of course the division into numbered chants is an important change in itself and one that has proved to be convenient for students, though it has also proved misleading.

A still more important change is in the title. By virtue of the image that holds the poem together, its title should be "Leaves of Grass," but Whitman had transferred this phrase to the book as a whole. In the first edition, the frontispiece partly takes the place of a title, since readers are being asked to interpret the poem as the testament of the idealized American workingman whom it portrays. In the second or 1856 edition, there is a title in words: "A Poem of Walt Whitman, an American." That is an awkward but accurate phrase, if we regard Walt (not Walter) Whitman as the name of the idealized figure. Beginning with the third or 1860 edition, the poem was called simply "Walt Whitman"—not so accurate a title any longer, if we remember that the name was by now completely identified with the living poet. It was not until 1881 that the poem became "Song of Myself," a phrase that I think is completely false to its original intention. "Myself" is "my personality," and Whitman had originally been writing about a not-myself, a representative figure who, by achieving union with his transpersonal soul, had realized the possibilities latent in every man and woman.

In the first edition the poet-hero presents himself, as I said, without a hint of his local or family background; he is simply "Walt Whitman, an American, one of the roughs, a kosmos." That is exactly how he should be presented, since he is speaking for all Americans and indeed for all humanity. In later editions he acquires a personal background by virtue of his complete identification with the author. As "Walt Whitman, a kosmos, of Manhattan the son," he becomes a strictly localized divinity (while ceasing to imply that each of the roughs contains in himself the entire universe). There are other changes in the same direction. In 1881 Whitman took eight lines from "Starting from Paumanok," which was written in his beatnik days, and inserted them at the end of the first chant. Four of the new lines are:

> My tongue, every atom of my blood, form'd from this soil, this air,
> Born here of parents born here from parents the same, and their
>   parents the same,
> I, now thirty-seven years old in perfect health begin,
> Hoping to cease not till death.

He was actually thirty-four or -five when he started to write the poem, and thirty-six when it was published—but what does it matter about his age or health or his determination to cease not till death? The real point is that if he insists on presenting himself as a proud descendant of the early settlers, he can no longer presume to speak for first-generation Americans; nor can he claim to be "Not merely of the New World but of Africa, Europe or Asia. . . . a wandering savage," as he had done in the original text. He has gained an identity at the cost of ceasing to be universally representative.

There is a significant change in the first line of the poem, the addition (in 1881) of three words I have put in italics: "I celebrate myself, *and sing myself*." At first one feels that "celebrate" and "sing" are synonyms, and that the new phrase has been added partly to balance the line and partly in obedience to Whitman's old-age habit of never saying in three words what might be said in six. But the truth is that "sing" introduces a new theme into the text. In the first edition the poet-hero had "celebrated" himself by telling what he saw and did and believed. He had spoken compulsively and without self-conscious-ness. In the late editions, however, he also "sings"—which in Whitman's jargon means "writes a song about"—himself. When he observes the miraculous world about him, it is no longer for the pure joy of seeing, as in the first edition, but also with the intention of collecting material; he is "Absorbing all to myself and for this song." This new habit of his becomes particularly obtrusive at the beginning of chant 26. Here, in the original version, the poet-hero had been preparing to demonstrate that by merely listening, in a state of complete passivity, he could be swept forward into an ecstasy of hearing. He had said in the first two lines:

> I think I will do nothing for a long time but listen,
> And accrue what I hear into myself. . . . and let sounds contribute
>   toward me.

Only four words of the second line were changed in 1881, but they were important for the meaning. The new line reads (with my italics):

> *To* accrue what I hear into *this song, to* let sounds contribute
>   toward *it*.

"To" implies purpose here: "in order to." If the poet is consciously trying to hear sounds that will enrich the texture of his song, he is no longer being passive, and the effect on the reader of the passage that follows is seriously weakened.

The good gray poet must have been abashed by many gestures of his earlier myself. "Washes and razors for foofoos. . . . for me freckles and a bristling beard." One can be certain that such a line would go; the wonder is that it survived until 1881. "Where the laughing gull scoots by the slappy shore and laughs her near-human laugh." The word "slappy" gives color to the line, and it was the one word to be omitted, in this case as early as 1856. There is no space to offer more than this bare suggestion of all the gay impudence and vivid Yankee-isms that were excised from later editions. I am more interested at present in apparently minor revisions that change the meaning of the poem. Among them are the phrases that introduce his accounts of the Goliad massacre in Texas (chant 34) and of the sea fight between the

Serapis and the *Bonhomme Richard* (chants 35 and 36). In the first edition these two accounts are offered as further examples of the power of identification. The poet-hero *is* one of the murdered Texans—perhaps the "youth not seventeen years old"— and he *is* one of the sailors on the *Bonhomme Richard*, just as he had already been the mother condemned for a witch and the hounded slave that flagged in the race. By 1867, however, Whitman felt he should offer explanations. He inserted a line at the beginning of chant 34, "Now I tell what I knew in Texas in my early youth," thus falsifying his own biography, and he inserted another line at the end of the first stanza of chant 35, besides two words, which I have italicized, in the first line of the following stanza:

List to the yarn, as my grandmother's father the sailor told it to me.

Our foe was no skulk in his ship I tell you (*said he,*)

The result is that these great examples of the poet-hero's ability to identify himself with all creatures, living or dead, are reduced in one case to a story told long ago in Texas, in the other to an old sailor's yarn—"said he"—and thereby lose their reason for being part of the poem. Whitman can no longer say about them, "I am the man. . . . I suffered. . . . I was there." In both cases it would seem, however, that he was not so much concealing what he once meant to say as, on this occasion, honestly forgetting it.

I have been talking about the revisions only in "Song of Myself," but some of the same statements could be made about the final text of the other eleven poems in the first edition. Since these poems are less important, the revisions in them seem less objectionable. "Song of the Answerer" and "Who Learns My Lesson Complete?" were improved, even greatly improved, by the omission from each of tasteless lines and a feeble ending. "Great Are the Myths," a still weaker poem, disappeared after 1876 without being missed. On the other hand, two of the best poems suffered most from revision: "The Sleepers" by losing a passage (lines 60–70) that starts with adolescent sex and ends in surrealism, and "I Sing the Body Electric" by the addition of a final section that is not in the least electric, being merely a long anatomical catalogue.

In another sense, however, all the poems have suffered, even those in which the revision was wisely handled. Most of them had been composed at the same time, in the same furious burst of inspiration; the only exceptions seem to be the two political poems, "Europe the 72d and 73d Years of These States," written in 1850—it was Whitman's first successful experiment in free verse—and "A Boston Ballad," written in June 1854. The other poems all have something to do with his state of mystical illumination; they explain one another, strengthen one another, and are further strengthened by being printed after "Song of Myself," since they amplify some of the same themes. In the text of the Deathbed edition, ten of them are scattered among six of the "clusters" into which the book was finally divided, while "Song of Myself" is paired with the vastly inflated "Starting from Paumanok." It is as if a close family of brothers had been assigned to separate branches of the armed forces, with the result that each of them lost something of his personality without contributing much to his new group. In the first edition everything belongs together and everything helps to exhibit Whitman at his best, Whitman at his freshest in vision and boldest in language, Whitman transformed by a new experience, so that he wanders among familiar objects and finds that each of them has become a miracle. One can read the book today with something of the amazement and the gratitude for its great power that Emerson felt when reading it more than a century ago.

A word about the text as reprinted in this volume. It follows the first edition faithfully, including Whitman's peculiarities of spelling, but I did not think it necessary to reproduce the typographical errors that he overlooked when reading proof. The test of a typographical error is whether it was corrected in the succeeding editions, especially the third, which was carefully printed. Thus, "abode" for "adobe" ("Song of Myself," line 320) was a typographical error and was corrected in the 1860 edition to "adobie," which ranks as a peculiarity of spelling, like the famous "loafe." I have supplied Whitman's final titles for the poems, but of course have put them in square brackets. The division into numbered chants is something I should have liked to omit. It isn't found in the first edition, it interferes with the unified movement of the poems—especially "Song of Myself"—but it also offers the only practical means of referring from one edition to another. The compromise I found was to print the chant numbers unobtrusively at the left margin, also in square brackets. Among Whitman scholars I should especially like to thank Gay Wilson Allen for assembling so many verified facts in usable form, and James E. Miller, Jr., for his illuminating study of "Song of Myself"—even though he will find that I disagree with him on almost everything but his central point.

MALCOLM COWLEY

LEAVES OF GRASS

The First (1855) Edition

Leaves

of

Grass.

———◦———

Brooklyn, New York:
1855.

AMERICA does not repel the past or what it has produced under its forms or amid other politics or the idea of castes or the old religions . . . accepts the lesson with calmness . . . is not so impatient as has been supposed that the slough still sticks to opinions and manners and literature while the life which served its requirements has passed into the new life of the new forms . . . perceives that the corpse is slowly borne from the eating and sleeping rooms of the house . . . perceives that it waits a little while in the door . . . that it was fittest for its days . . . that its action has descended to the stalwart and wellshaped heir who approaches . . . and that he shall be fittest for his days.

The Americans of all nations at any time upon the earth have probably the fullest poetical nature. The United States themselves are essentially the greatest poem. In the history of the earth hitherto the largest and most stirring appear tame and orderly to their ampler largeness and stir. Here at last is something in the doings of man that corresponds with the broadcast doings of the day and night. Here is not merely a nation but a teeming nation of nations. Here is action untied from strings necessarily blind to particulars and details magnificently moving in vast masses. Here is the hospitality which forever indicates heroes. . . . Here are the roughs and beards and space and ruggedness and nonchalance that the soul loves. Here the performance disdaining the trivial unapproached in the tremendous audacity of its crowds and groupings and the push of its perspective spreads with crampless and flowing breadth and showers its prolific and splendid extravagance. One sees it must indeed own the riches of the summer and winter, and need never be bankrupt while corn grows from the ground or the orchards drop apples or the bays contain fish or men beget children upon women.

Other states indicate themselves in their deputies . . . but the genius of the United States is not best or most in its executives or legislatures, nor in its ambassadors or authors or colleges or churches or parlors, nor even in its newspapers or inventors . . . but always most in the common people. Their manners speech dress friendships—the freshness and candor of their physiognomy—the picturesque looseness of their carriage . . . their death-less attachment to freedom—their aversion to anything indecorous or soft or mean—the practical acknowledgment of the citizens of one state by the citizens of all other states—the fierceness of their roused resentment—their curiosity and welcome of novelty—their self-esteem and wonderful sym-pathy—their susceptibility to a slight—the air they have of persons who never knew how it felt to stand in the presence of superiors—the fluency of their speech—their delight in music, the sure symptom of manly tenderness and native elegance of soul . . . their good temper and openhandedness— the terrible significance of their elections—the President's taking off his hat to them not they to him—these too are unrhymed poetry. It awaits the gigantic and generous treatment worthy of it.

The largeness of nature of the nation were monstrous without a cor-responding largeness and generosity of the spirit of the citizen. Not nature nor swarming states nor streets and steamships nor prosperous business nor farms nor capital nor learning may suffice for the ideal of man . . . nor suffice the poet. No reminiscences may suffice either. A live nation can always cut a deep mark and can have the best authority the cheapest . . . namely from its own soul. This is the sum of the profitable uses of individuals or states and of present action and grandeur and of the subjects of poets.— As if it were necessary to trot back generation after generation to the eastern records! As if the beauty and sacredness of the demonstrable must fall be-hind that of the mythical! As if men do not make their mark out of any times! As if the opening of the western continent by discovery and what has transpired since in North and South America were less than the small theatre of the antique or the aimless sleepwalking of the middle ages! The pride of the United States leaves the wealth and finesse of the cities and all returns of commerce and agriculture and all the magnitude of geography or shows of exterior victory to enjoy the breed of fullsized men or one full-sized man unconquerable and simple.

The American poets are to enclose old and new for America is the race of races. Of them a bard is to be commensurate with a people. To him the other continents arrive as contributions . . . he gives them reception for their sake and his own sake. His spirit responds to his country's spirit . . . he incarnates its geography and natural life and rivers and lakes. Mississippi with annual freshets and changing chutes, Missouri and Columbia and Ohio and Saint Lawrence with the falls and beautiful masculine Hudson, do not embouchure where they spend themselves more than they embouchure into him. The blue breadth over the inland sea of Virginia and Maryland and the sea off Massachusetts and Maine and over Manhattan bay and over Champlain and Erie and over Ontario and Huron and Michigan and Superior, and over the Texan and Mexican and Floridian and Cuban seas and over the seas off California and Oregon, is not tallied by the blue breadth of the waters below more than the breadth of above and below is tallied by him. When the long Atlantic coast stretches longer and the Pacific coast stretches longer he easily stretches with them north or south. He spans between them also from east to west and reflects what is between them. On him rise solid growths that offset the growths of pine and cedar and hemlock and liveoak and locust and chestnut and cypress and hickory and limetree and cotton-wood and tuliptree and cactus and wildvine and tamarind and persimmon . . . and tangles as tangled as any canebrake or swamp . . . and forests coated with transparent ice and icicles hanging from the boughs and crackling in the wind . . . and sides and peaks of mountains . . . and pasturage sweet and free as savannah or upland or prairie . . . with flights and songs and screams that answer those of the wildpigeon and highhold and orchard-oriole and coot and surf-duck and redshouldered-hawk and fish-hawk and white-ibis and indian-hen and cat-owl and water-pheasant and qua-bird and pied-sheldrake and blackbird and mockingbird and buzzard and condor and night-heron and eagle. To him the hereditary countenance descends both mother's and father's. To him enter the essences of the real things and past and present events—of the enormous diversity of temperature and agriculture and mines—the tribes of red aborigines—the weatherbeaten vessels entering new ports or making landings on rocky coasts—the first settlements north or south—the rapid stature and muscle—the haughty defiance of '76, and the war and peace and formation of the constitution . . . the union always surrounded by blatherers and always calm and impregnable—the perpetual coming of immigrants—the wharfhem'd cities and superior marine—the unsurveyed interior—the loghouses and clearings and wild animals and hunters and trappers . . . the free commerce—the fisheries and whaling and gold-digging—the endless gestation of new states

—the convening of Congress every December, the members duly coming up from all climates and the uttermost parts . . . the noble character of the young mechanics and of all free American workmen and workwomen . . . the general ardor and friendliness and enterprise—the perfect equality of the female with the male . . . the large amativeness—the fluid movement of the population—the factories and mercantile life and laborsaving machinery—the Yankee swap—the New-York firemen and the target excursion—the southern plantation life—the character of the northeast and of the northwest and southwest—slavery and the tremulous spreading of hands to protect it, and the stern opposition to it which shall never cease till it ceases or the speaking of tongues and the moving of lips cease. For such the expression of the American poet is to be transcendent and new. It is to be indirect and not direct or descriptive or epic. Its quality goes through these to much more. Let the age and wars of other nations be chanted and their eras and characters be illustrated and that finish the verse. Not so the great psalm of the republic. Here the theme is creative and has vista. Here comes one among the wellbeloved stonecutters and plans with decision and science and sees the solid and beautiful forms of the future where there are now no solid forms.

Of all nations the United States with veins full of poetical stuff most need poets and will doubtless have the greatest and use them the greatest. Their Presidents shall not be their common referee so much as their poets shall. Of all mankind the great poet is the equable man. Not in him but off from him things are grotesque or eccentric or fail of their sanity. Nothing out of its place is good and nothing in its place is bad. He bestows on every object or quality its fit proportions neither more nor less. He is the arbiter of the diverse and he is the key. He is the equalizer of his age and land . . . he supplies what wants supplying and checks what wants checking. If peace is the routine out of him speaks the spirit of peace, large, rich, thrifty, building vast and populous cities, encouraging agriculture and the arts and commerce—lighting the study of man, the soul, immortality—federal, state or municipal government, marriage, health, freetrade, intertravel by land and sea . . . nothing too close, nothing too far off . . . the stars not too far off. In war he is the most deadly force of the war. Who recruits him recruits horse and foot . . . he fetches parks of artillery the best that engineer ever knew. If the time becomes slothful and heavy he knows how to arouse it . . . he can make every word he speaks draw blood. Whatever stagnates in the flat of custom or obedience or legislation he never stagnates. Obedience does not master him, he masters it. High up out of reach he stands turning a concentrated light . . . he turns the pivot with his finger . . . he baffles the swiftest runners as he stands and easily overtakes and envelops them. The time straying toward infidelity and confections and persiflage he withholds by his steady faith . . . he spreads out his dishes . . . he offers the sweet firmfibred meat that grows men and women. His brain is the ultimate brain. He is no arguer . . . he is judgment. He judges not as the judge judges but as the sun falling around a helpless thing. As he sees the farthest he has the most faith. His thoughts are the hymns of the praise of things. In the talk on the soul and eternity and God off of his equal plane he is silent. He sees eternity less like a play with a prologue and denouement . . . he sees eternity in men and women . . . he does not see men and women as dreams or dots. Faith is the antiseptic of the soul . . . it pervades the common people and preserves them . . . they never give up believing and expecting and trusting. There is that indescribable freshness and unconsciousness about an illiterate person that humbles and mocks the power of the noblest expressive genius. The poet sees for a certainty how one not a great artist may be just as sacred and perfect as the greatest artist. . . . The power to destroy or remould is freely used by him but never the power of attack. What is past is past. If he does not expose superior models and prove himself by every step he takes he is not what is wanted. The presence of the greatest poet conquers . . . not parleying or struggling or any prepared attempts. Now he has passed that way see after him! there is not left any vestige of despair or misanthropy or cunning or exclusiveness or the ignominy of a nativity or color or delusion of hell or the necessity of hell . . . and no man thenceforward shall be degraded for ignorance or weakness or sin.

The greatest poet hardly knows pettiness or triviality. If he breathes into any thing that was before thought small it dilates with the grandeur and life of the universe. He is a seer . . . he is individual . . . he is complete in himself . . . the others are as good as he, only he sees it and they do not. He is not one of the chorus . . . he does not stop for any regulations . . . he is the president of regulation. What the eyesight does to the rest he does to the rest. Who knows the curious mystery of the eyesight? The other senses corroborate themselves, but this is removed from any proof but its own and foreruns the identities of the spiritual world. A single glance of it mocks all the investigations of man and all the instruments and books of the earth and all reasoning. What is marvellous? what is unlikely? what is impossible or baseless or vague? after you have once just opened the space of a peachpit and given audience to far and near and to the sunset and had all things enter with electric swiftness softly and duly without confusion or jostling or jam.

The land and sea, the animals fishes and birds, the sky of heaven and the orbs, the forests mountains and rivers, are not small themes . . . but folks expect of the poet to indicate more than the beauty and dignity which always attach to dumb real objects . . . they expect him to indicate the path between reality and their souls. Men and women perceive the beauty well enough . . . probably as well as he. The passionate tenacity of hunters, woodmen, early risers, cultivators of gardens and orchards and fields, the love of healthy women for the manly form, seafaring persons, drivers of horses, the passion for light and the open air, all is an old varied sign of the unfailing perception of beauty and of a residence of the poetic in outdoor people. They can never be assisted by poets to perceive . . . some may but they never can. The poetic quality is not marshalled in rhyme or uniformity or abstract addresses to things nor in melancholy complaints or good precepts, but is the life of these and much else and is in the soul. The profit of rhyme is that it drops seeds of a sweeter and more luxuriant rhyme, and of uniformity that it conveys itself into its own roots in the ground out of sight. The rhyme and uniformity of perfect poems show the free growth of metrical laws and bud from them as unerringly and loosely as lilacs or roses on a bush, and take shapes as compact as the shapes of chestnuts and oranges and melons and pears, and shed the perfume impalpable to form. The fluency and ornaments of the finest poems or music or orations or recitations are not independent but dependent. All beauty comes from beautiful blood and a beautiful brain. If the greatnesses are in conjunction in a man or woman it is enough . . . the fact will prevail through the universe . . . but the gaggery and gilt of a million years will not prevail. Who troubles himself about his ornaments or fluency is lost. This is what you shall do: Love the earth and sun and the animals, despise riches, give alms to every one that asks, stand up for the stupid and crazy, devote your income and labor to others, hate tyrants, argue not concerning God, have patience and indulgence toward the people, take off your hat to nothing known or unknown or to any man or number of men, go freely with powerful uneducated persons and with the young and with the mothers of families, read these leaves in the open air every season of every year of your life, re-examine all you have been told at school or church or in any book, dismiss whatever insults your own soul, and your very flesh shall be a great poem and have the richest fluency not only in its words but in the silent lines of its lips and face and between the lashes of your eyes and in every motion and joint of your body. . . . The poet shall not spend his time in unneeded work. He shall know that the ground is always ready ploughed and manured . . . others may not know it but he shall. He shall go directly to the creation. His trust shall master the trust of everything he touches . . . and shall master all attachment.

The known universe has one complete lover and that is the greatest poet. He consumes an eternal passion and is indifferent which chance happens and which possible contingency of fortune or misfortune and persuades daily and hourly his delicious pay. What balks or breaks others is fuel for his burning progress to contact and amorous joy. Other proportions of the reception of pleasure dwindle to nothing to his proportions. All expected from heaven or from the highest he is rapport with in the sight of the daybreak or a scene of the winter woods or the presence of children playing or with his arm round the neck of a man or woman. His love above all love has leisure and expanse . . . he leaves room ahead of himself. He is no irresolute or suspicious lover . . . he is sure . . . he scorns intervals. His experience and the showers and thrills are not for nothing. Nothing can jar him . . . suffering and darkness cannot—death and fear cannot. To him complaint and jealousy and envy are corpses buried and rotten in the earth . . . he saw them buried. The sea is not surer of the shore or the shore of the sea than he is of the fruition of his love and of all perfection and beauty.

The fruition of beauty is no chance of hit or miss . . . it is inevitable as life . . . it is exact and plumb as gravitation. From the eyesight proceeds another eyesight and from the hearing proceeds another hearing and from the voice proceeds another voice eternally curious of the harmony of things with man. To these respond perfections not only in the committees that were supposed to stand for the rest but in the rest themselves just the same. These understand the law of perfection in masses and floods . . . that its finish is to each for itself and onward from itself . . . that it is profuse and impartial . . . that there is not a minute of the light or dark nor an acre of the earth or sea without it—nor any direction of the sky nor any trade or employment nor any turn of events. This is the reason that about the proper expression of beauty there is precision and balance . . . one part does not need to be thrust above another. The best singer is not the one who has the most lithe and powerful organ . . . the pleasure of poems is not in them that take the handsomest measure and similes and sound.

Without effort and without exposing in the least how it is done the greatest poet brings the spirit of any or all events and passions and scenes and persons some more and some less to bear on your individual character as you hear or read. To do this well is to compete with the laws that pursue and follow time. What is the purpose must surely be there and the clue of it must be there . . . and the faintest indication is the indication of the best and then becomes the clearest indication. Past and present and future are not disjoined but joined. The greatest poet forms the consistence of what is to be from what has been and is. He drags the dead out of their coffins and stands them again on their feet . . . he says to the past, Rise and walk before me that I may realize you. He learns the lesson . . . he places himself where the future becomes present. The greatest poet does not only dazzle his rays over character and scenes and passions . . . he finally ascends and finishes all . . . he exhibits the pinnacles that no man can tell what they are for or what is beyond . . . he glows a moment on the extremest verge. He is most wonderful in his last half-hidden smile or frown . . . by that flash of the moment of parting the one that sees it shall be encouraged or terrified afterwards for many years. The greatest poet does not moralize or make applications of morals . . . he knows the soul. The soul has that measureless pride which consists in never acknowledging any lessons but its own. But it has sympathy as measureless as its pride and the one balances the other and neither can stretch too far while it stretches in company with the other. The inmost secrets of art sleep with the twain. The greatest poet has lain close betwixt both and they are vital in his style and thoughts.

The art of art, the glory of expression and the sunshine of the light of letters is simplicity. Nothing is better than simplicity . . . nothing can make up for excess or for the lack of definiteness. To carry on the heave of impulse and pierce intellectual depths and give all subjects their articulations are powers neither common nor very uncommon. But to speak in literature with the perfect rectitude and insouciance of the movements of animals and the unimpeachableness of the sentiment of trees in the woods and grass by the roadside is the flawless triumph of art. If you have looked on him who has achieved it you have looked on one of the masters of the artists of all nations and times. You shall not contemplate the flight of the graygull over the bay or the mettlesome action of the blood horse or the tall leaning of sunflowers on their stalk or the appearance of the sun journeying through heaven or the appearance of the moon afterward with any more satisfaction than you shall contemplate him. The greatest poet has less a marked style and is more the channel of thoughts and things without increase or diminution, and is the free channel of himself. He swears to his art, I will not be meddlesome, I will not have in my writing any elegance or effect or originality to hang in the way between me and the rest like curtains. I will have nothing hang in the way, not the richest curtains. What I tell I tell for precisely what it is. Let who may exalt or startle or fascinate or soothe I will have purposes as health or heat or snow has and be as regardless of observation. What I experience or portray shall go from my composition without a shred of my composition. You shall stand by my side and look in the mirror with me.

The old red blood and stainless gentility of great poets will be proved by their unconstraint. A heroic person walks at his ease through and out of that custom or precedent or authority that suits him not. Of the traits of the brotherhood of writers savans musicians inventors and artists nothing is finer than silent defiance advancing from new free forms. In the need of poems philosophy politics mechanism science behaviour, the craft of art, an appropriate native grand-opera, shipcraft, or any craft, he is greatest forever and forever who contributes the greatest original practical example. The cleanest expression is that which finds no sphere worthy of itself and makes one.

The messages of great poets to each man and woman are, Come to us on equal terms, Only then can you understand us, We are no better than you, What we enclose you enclose, What we enjoy you may enjoy. Did you suppose there could be only one Supreme? We affirm there can be unnumbered Supremes, and that one does not countervail another any more than one eyesight countervails another . . . and that men can be good or grand only of the consciousness of their supremacy within them. What do you think is the grandeur of storms and dismemberments and the deadliest battles and wrecks and the wildest fury of the elements and the power of the sea and the motion of nature and of the throes of human desires and dignity and hate and love? It is that something in the soul which says, Rage on, Whirl on, I tread master here and everywhere, Master of the spasms of the sky and of the shatter of the sea, Master of nature and passion and death, And of all terror and all pain.

The American bards shall be marked for generosity and affection and for encouraging competitors . . . They shall be kosmos . . . without monopoly or secrecy . . . glad to pass any thing to any one . . . hungry for equals night and day. They shall not be careful of riches and privilege . . . they shall be riches and privilege . . . they shall perceive who the most affluent man is. The most affluent man is he that confronts all the shows he sees by equivalents out of the stronger wealth of himself. The American bard shall delineate no class of persons nor one or two out of the strata of interests nor love most nor truth most nor the soul most nor the body most . . . and not be for the eastern states more than the western or the northern states more than the southern.

Exact science and its practical movements are no checks on the greatest poet but always his encouragement and support. The outset and remembrance are there . . . there the arms that lifted him first and brace him best . . . there he returns after all his goings and comings. The sailor and traveler . . . the anatomist chemist astronomer geologist phrenologist spiritualist mathematician historian and lexicographer are not poets, but they are the lawgivers of poets and their construction underlies the structure of every perfect poem. No matter what rises or is uttered they sent the seed of the conception of it . . . of them and by them stand the visible proofs of souls . . . always of their fatherstuff must be begotten the sinewy races of bards. If there shall be love and content between the father and the son and if the greatness of the son is the exuding of the greatness of the father there shall be love between the poet and the man of demonstrable science. In the beauty of poems are the tuft and final applause of science.

Great is the faith of the flush of knowledge and of the investigation of the depths of qualities and things. Cleaving and circling here swells the soul of the poet yet is president of itself always. The depths are fathomless and therefore calm. The innocence and nakedness are resumed . . . they are neither modest nor immodest. The whole theory of the special and supernatural and all that was twined with it or educed out of it departs as a dream. What has ever happened . . . what happens and whatever may or shall happen, the vital laws enclose all . . . they are sufficient for any case and for all cases . . . none to be hurried or retarded . . . any miracle of affairs or persons inadmissible in the vast clear scheme where every motion and every spear of grass and the frames and spirits of men and women and all that concerns them are unspeakably perfect miracles all referring to all and each distinct and in its place. It is also not consistent with the reality of the soul to admit that there is anything in the known universe more divine than men and women.

Men and women and the earth and all upon it are simply to be taken as they are, and the investigation of their past and present and future shall be unintermitted and shall be done with perfect candor. Upon this basis philosophy speculates ever looking toward the poet, ever regarding the eternal tendencies of all toward happiness never inconsistent with what is clear to the senses and to the soul. For the eternal tendencies of all toward happiness make the only point of sane philosophy. Whatever comprehends less than that . . . whatever is less than the laws of light and of astronomical motion . . . or less than the laws that follow the thief the liar the glutton and the drunkard through this life and doubtless afterward . . . or less than vast stretches of time or the slow formation of density or the patient up-heaving of strata —is of no account. Whatever would put God in a poem or system of philosophy as contending against some being or influence is also of no account. Sanity and ensemble characterise the great master . . . spoilt in one principle all is spoilt. The great master has nothing to do with miracles. He sees health for himself in being one of the mass . . . he sees the hiatus in singular eminence. To the perfect shape comes common ground. To be under the general law is great for that is to correspond with it. The master knows that he is unspeakably great and that all are unspeakably great . . . that nothing for instance is greater than to conceive children and bring them up well . . . that to be is just as great as to perceive or tell.

In the make of the great masters the idea of political liberty is indispensable. Liberty takes the adherence of heroes wherever men and women exist . . . but never takes any adherence or welcome from the rest more than from poets. They are the voice and exposition of liberty. They out of ages are worthy the grand idea . . . to them it is confided and they must sustain it. Nothing has precedence of it and nothing can warp or degrade it. The attitude of great poets is to cheer up slaves and horrify despots. The turn of their necks, the sound of their feet, the motions of their wrists, are full of hazard to the one and hope to the other. Come nigh them awhile and though they neither speak or advise you shall learn the faithful American lesson.

Liberty is poorly served by men whose good intent is quelled from one failure or two failures or any number of failures, or from the casual indifference or ingratitude of the people, or from the sharp show of the tushes of power, or the bringing to bear soldiers and cannon or any penal statutes. Liberty relies upon itself, invites no one, promises nothing, sits in calmness and light, is positive and composed, and knows no discouragement. The battle rages with many a loud alarm and frequent advance and retreat . . . the enemy triumphs . . . the prison, the handcuffs, the iron necklace and anklet, the scaffold, garrote and leadballs do their work . . . the cause is asleep . . . the strong throats are choked with their own blood . . . the young men drop their eyelashes toward the ground when they pass each other . . . and is liberty gone out of that place? No never. When liberty goes it is not the first to go nor the second or third to go . . . it waits for all the rest to go . . . it is the last . . . When the memories of the old martyrs are faded utterly away . . . when the large names of patriots are laughed at in the public halls from the lips of the orators . . . when the boys are no more christened after the same but christened after tyrants and traitors instead . . . when the laws of the free are grudgingly permitted and laws for informers and bloodmoney are sweet to the taste of the people . . . when I and you walk abroad upon the earth stung with compassion at the sight of numberless brothers answering our equal friendship and calling no man master—and when we are elated with noble joy at the sight of slaves . . . when the soul retires in the cool communion of the night and surveys its experience and has much extasy over the word and deed that put back a helpless innocent person into the gripe of the gripers or into any cruel inferiority . . . when those in all parts of these states who could easier realize the true American character but do not yet—when the swarms of cringers, suckers, dough-faces, lice of politics, planners of sly involutions for their own preferment to city offices or state legislatures or the judiciary or congress or the presidency, obtain a response of love and natural deference from the people whether they get the offices or no . . . when it is better to be a bound booby and rogue in office at a high salary than the poorest free mechanic or farmer with his hat unmoved from his head and firm eyes and a candid and generous heart . . . and when servility by town or state or the federal government or any oppression on a large scale or small scale can be tried on without its own punishment following duly after in exact proportion against the smallest chance of escape . . . or rather when all life and all the souls of men and women are discharged from any part of the earth—then only shall the instinct of liberty be discharged from that part of the earth.

As the attributes of the poets of the kosmos concentre in the real body and soul and in the pleasure of things they possess the superiority of genuineness over all fiction and romance. As they emit themselves facts are showered over with light . . . the daylight is lit with more volatile light . . . also the deep between the setting and rising sun goes deeper many fold. Each precise object or condition or combination or process exhibits a beauty . . . the multiplication table its—old age its—the carpenter's trade its— the grand-opera its . . . the hugehulled cleanshaped New-York clipper at sea under steam or full sail gleams with unmatched beauty . . . the American circles and large harmonies of government gleam with theirs . . . and the commonest definite intentions and actions with theirs. The poets of the kosmos advance through all interpositions and coverings and turmoils and stratagems to first principles. They are of use . . . they dissolve poverty from its need and riches from its conceit. You large proprietor they say shall not realize or perceive more than any one else. The owner of the library is not he who holds a legal title to it having bought and paid for it. Any one and every one is owner of the library who can read the same through all the varieties of tongues and subjects and styles, and in whom they enter with ease and take residence and force toward paternity and maternity, and make supple and powerful and rich and large. . . . These American states strong and healthy and accomplished shall receive no pleasure from violations of natural models and must not permit them. In paintings or mouldings or carvings in mineral or wood, or in the illustrations of books or newspapers, or in any comic or tragic prints, or in the patterns of woven stuffs or any thing to beautify rooms or furniture or costumes, or to put upon cornices or monuments or on the prows or sterns of ships, or to put anywhere before the human eye indoors or out, that which distorts honest shapes or which creates unearthly beings or places or contingencies is a nuisance and revolt. Of the human form especially it is so great it must never be made ridiculous. Of ornaments to a work nothing outre can be allowed . . . but those ornaments can be allowed that conform to the perfect facts of the open air and that flow out of the nature of the work and come irrepressibly from it and are necessary to the completion of the work. Most works are most beautiful without ornament. . . . Exaggerations will be revenged in human physiology. Clean and vigorous children are jetted and conceived only in those communities where the models of natural forms are public every day. . . . Great genius and the people of these states must never be demeaned to romances. As soon as histories are properly told there is no more need of romances.

The great poets are also to be known by the absence in them of tricks and by the justification of perfect personal candor. Then folks echo a new cheap joy and a divine voice leaping from their brains: How beautiful is candor! All faults may be forgiven of him who has perfect candor. Henceforth let no man of us lie, for we have seen that openness wins the inner and outer world and that there is no single exception, and that never since our earth gathered itself in a mass have deceit or subterfuge or prevarication attracted its smallest particle or the faintest tinge of a shade—and that through the enveloping wealth and rank of a state or the whole republic of states a sneak or sly person shall be discovered and despised . . . and that the soul has never been once fooled and never can be fooled . . . and thrift without the loving nod of the soul is only a fœtid puff . . . and there never grew up in any of the continents of the globe nor upon any planet or satellite or star, nor upon the asteroids, nor in any part of ethereal space, nor in the midst of density, nor under the fluid wet of the sea, nor in that condition which precedes the birth of babes, nor at any time during the changes of life, nor in that condition that follows what we term death, nor in any stretch of abeyance or action afterward of vitality, nor in any process of formation or reformation anywhere, a being whose instinct hated the truth.

Extreme caution or prudence, the soundest organic health, large hope and comparison and fondness for women and children, large alimentiveness and destructiveness and causality, with a perfect sense of the oneness of nature and the propriety of the same spirit applied to human affairs . . . these are called up of the float of the brain of the world to be parts of the greatest poet from his birth out of his mother's womb and from her birth out of her mother's. Caution seldom goes far enough. It has been thought that the prudent citizen was the citizen who applied himself to solid gains and did well for himself and his family and completed a lawful life without debt or crime. The greatest poet sees and admits these economies as he sees the economies of food and sleep, but has higher notions of prudence than to think he gives much when he gives a few slight attentions at the latch of the gate. The premises of the prudence of life are not the hospitality of it or the ripeness and harvest of it. Beyond the independence of a little sum laid

aside for burial-money, and of a few clapboards around and shingles
overhead on a lot of American soil owned, and the easy dollars that supply
the year's plain clothing and meals, the melancholy prudence of the aban-
donment of such a great being as a man is to the toss and pallor of years of
moneymaking with all their scorching days and icy nights and all their
stifling deceits and underhanded dodgings, or infinitesimals of parlors, or
shameless stuffing while others starve . . . and all the loss of the bloom and
odor of the earth and of the flowers and atmosphere and of the sea and of
the true taste of the women and men you pass or have to do with in youth
or middle age, and the issuing sickness and desperate revolt at the close of
a life without elevation or naivete, and the ghastly chatter of a death
without serenity or majesty, is the great fraud upon modern civilization
and forethought, blotching the surface and system which civilization un-
deniably drafts, and moistening with tears the immense features it spreads
and spreads with such velocity before the reached kisses of the soul . . .
Still the right explanation remains to be made about prudence. The prudence of the mere wealth and respectability of the most esteemed life appears too faint for the eye to observe at all when little and large alike drop
quietly aside at the thought of the prudence suitable for immortality. What
is wisdom that fills the thinness of a year or seventy or eighty years to wisdom spaced out by ages and coming back at a certain time with strong
reinforcements and rich presents and the clear faces of wedding-guests as
far as you can look in every direction running gaily toward you? Only the
soul is of itself . . . all else has reference to what ensues. All that a person
does or thinks is of consequence. Not a move can a man or woman make
that affects him or her in a day or a month or any part of the direct lifetime
or the hour of death but the same affects him or her onward afterward
through the indirect lifetime. The indirect is always as great and real as
the direct. The spirit receives from the body just as much as it gives to the
body. Not one name of word or deed . . . not of venereal sores or discolora-
tions . . . not the privacy of the onanist . . . not of the putrid veins of gluttons
or rumdrinkers . . . not peculation or cunning or betrayal or murder . . .
no serpentine poison of those that seduce women . . . not the foolish yielding
of women . . . not prostitution . . . not of any depravity of young men . . .
not of the attainment of gain by discreditable means . . . not any nastiness
of appetite . . . not any harshness of officers to men or judges to prisoners or
fathers to sons or sons to fathers or husbands to wives or bosses to their boys

. . . not of greedy looks or malignant wishes . . . nor any of the wiles practised by people upon themselves . . . ever is or ever can be stamped on the programme but it is duly realized and returned, and that returned in further performances . . . and they returned again. Nor can the push of charity or personal force ever be any thing else then the profoundest reason, whether it brings arguments to hand or no. No specification is necessary . . . to add or subtract or divide is in vain. Little or big, learned or unlearned, white or black, legal or illegal, sick or well, from the first inspiration down the windpipe to the last expiration out of it, all that a male or female does that is vigorous and benevolent and clean is so much sure profit to him or her in the unshakable order of the universe and through the whole scope of it forever. If the savage or felon is wise it is well . . . if the greatest poet or savan is wise it is simply the same . . . if the President or chief justice is wise it is the same . . . if the young mechanic or farmer is wise it is no more or less . . . if the prostitute is wise it is no more nor less. The interest will come round . . . all will come round. All the best actions of war and peace . . . all help given to relatives and strangers and the poor and old and sorrowful and young children and widows and the sick, and to all shunned persons . . . all furtherance of fugitives and of the escape of slaves . . . all the self-denial that stood steady and aloof on wrecks and saw others take the seats of the boats . . . all offering of substance or life for the good old cause, or for a friend's sake or opinion's sake . . . all pains of enthusiasts scoffed at by their neighbors . . . all the vast sweet love and precious suffering of mothers . . . all honest men baffled in strifes recorded or unrecorded . . . all the grandeur and good of the few ancient nations whose fragments of annals we inherit . . . and all the good of the hundreds of far mightier and more ancient nations unknown to us by name or date or location . . . all that was ever manfully begun, whether it succeeded or not . . . all that has at any time been well suggested out of the divine heart of man or by the divinity of his mouth or by the shaping of his great hands . . . and all that is well thought or done this day on any part of the surface of the globe . . . or on any of the wandering stars or fixed stars by those there as we are here . . . or that is henceforth to be well thought or done by you whoever you are, or by any one—these singly and wholly inured at their time and inure now and will inure always to the identities from which they sprung or shall spring . . . Did you guess any of them lived only its moment? The world does not so exist . . . no parts palpable or impalpable so exist . . . no result exists now without being from its long antecedent result, and that from its antecedent, and so backward without the farthest mentionable spot coming a bit nearer the beginning than any other spot. . . . Whatever satisfies the soul is truth. The prudence of the greatest poet answers at last the craving and glut of the soul, is not contemptuous of less ways of prudence if they conform to its ways, puts off nothing, permits no let-up for its own case or any case, has no particular sabbath or judgment-day, divides not the living from the dead or the righteous from the unrighteous, is satisfied with the present, matches every thought or act by its correlative, knows no possible forgiveness or deputed atonement . . . knows that the young man who composedly periled his life and lost it has done exceeding well for himself, while the man who has not periled his life and retains it to old age in riches and ease has perhaps achieved nothing for himself worth mentioning . . . and that only that person has no great prudence to learn who has learnt to prefer real longlived things, and favors body and soul the same, and perceives the indirect assuredly following the direct, and what evil or good he does leaping onward and waiting to meet him again—and who in his spirit in any emergency whatever neither hurries or avoids death.

The direct trial of him who would be the greatest poet is today. If he does not flood himself with the immediate age as with vast oceanic tides . . . and if he does not attract his own land body and soul to himself and hang on its neck with incomparable love and plunge his semitic muscle into its merits and demerits . . . and if he be not himself the age transfigured . . . and if to him is not opened the eternity which gives similitude to all periods and locations and processes and animate and inanimate forms, and which is the bond of time, and rises up from its inconceivable vagueness and infiniteness in the swimming shape of today, and is held by the ductile anchors of life, and makes the present spot the passage from what was to what shall be, and commits itself to the representation of this wave of an hour and this one of the sixty beautiful children of the wave—let him merge in the general run and wait his development. . . . Still the final test of poems or any character or work remains. The prescient poet projects himself centuries ahead and judges performer or performance after the changes of time. Does it live through them? Does it still hold on untired? Will the same style and the direction of genius to similar points be satisfactory now? Has no new discovery in science or arrival at superior planes of thought and judgment and behaviour fixed him or his so that either can be looked down upon? Have the marches of tens and hundreds and thousands of years made willing detours to the right hand and the left hand for his sake? Is he beloved long and long after he is buried? Does the young man think often of him? and the young woman think often of him? and do the middleaged and the old think of him?

A great poem is for ages and ages in common and for all degrees and complexions and all departments and sects and for a woman as much as a man and a man as much as a woman. A great poem is no finish to a man or woman but rather a beginning. Has any one fancied he could sit at last under some due authority and rest satisfied with explanations and realize and be content and full? To no such terminus does the greatest poet bring . . . he brings neither cessation or sheltered fatness and ease. The touch of him tells in action. Whom he takes he takes with firm sure grasp into live regions previously unattained . . . thenceforward is no rest . . . they see the space and ineffable sheen that turn the old spots and lights into dead vacuums. The companion of him beholds the birth and progress of stars and learns one of the meanings. Now there shall be a man cohered out of tumult and chaos . . . the elder encourages the younger and shows him how . . . they two shall launch off fearlessly together till the new world fits an orbit for itself and looks unabashed on the lesser orbits of the stars and sweeps through the ceaseless rings and shall never be quiet again.

There will soon be no more priests. Their work is done. They may wait awhile . . . perhaps a generation or two . . . dropping off by degrees. A superior breed shall take their place . . . the gangs of kosmos and prophets en masse shall take their place. A new order shall arise and they shall be the priests of man, and every man shall be his own priest. The churches built under their umbrage shall be the churches of men and women. Through the divinity of themselves shall the kosmos and the new breed of poets be interpreters of men and women and of all events and things. They shall find their inspiration in real objects today, symptoms of the past and future. . . . They shall not deign to defend immortality or God or the perfection of things or liberty or the exquisite beauty and reality of the soul. They shall arise in America and be responded to from the remainder of the earth.

The English language befriends the grand American expression . . . it is brawny enough and limber and full enough. On the tough stock of a race who through all change of circumstances was never without the idea of political liberty, which is the animus of all liberty, it has attracted the terms of daintier and gayer and subtler and more elegant tongues. It is the powerful language of resistance . . . it is the dialect of common sense. It is the speech of the proud and melancholy races and of all who aspire. It is the chosen tongue to express growth faith self-esteem freedom justice equality friendliness amplitude prudence decision and courage. It is the medium that shall well nigh express the inexpressible.

No great literature nor any like style of behaviour or oratory or social intercourse or household arrangements or public institutions or the treatment by bosses of employed people, nor executive detail or detail of the army or navy, nor spirit of legislation or courts or police or tuition or architecture or songs or amusements or the costumes of young men, can long elude the jealous and passionate instinct of American standards. Whether or no the sign appears from the mouths of the people, it throbs a live interrogation in every freeman's and freewoman's heart after that which passes by or this built to remain. Is it uniform with my country? Are its disposals without ignominious distinctions? Is it for the evergrowing communes of brothers and lovers, large, well-united, proud beyond the old models, generous beyond all models? Is it something grown fresh out of the fields or drawn from the sea for use to me today here? I know that what answers for me an American must answer for any individual or nation that serves for a part of my materials. Does this answer? or is it without reference to universal needs? or sprung of the needs of the less developed society of special ranks? or old needs of pleasure overlaid by modern science and forms? Does this acknowledge liberty with audible and absolute acknowledgement, and set slavery at nought for life and death? Will it help breed one goodshaped and wellhung man, and a woman to be his perfect and independent mate? Does it improve manners? Is it for the nursing of the young of the republic? Does it solve readily with the sweet milk of the nipples of the breasts of the mother of many children? Has it too the old ever-fresh forbearance and impartiality? Does it look with the same love on the last born and on those hardening toward stature, and on the errant, and on those who disdain all strength of assault outside of their own?

The poems distilled from other poems will probably pass away. The coward will surely pass away. The expectation of the vital and great can only be satisfied by the demeanor of the vital and great.

The swarms of the polished deprecating and reflectors and the polite float off and leave no remembrance. America prepares with composure and goodwill for the visitors that have sent word. It is not intellect that is to be their warrant and welcome. The talented, the artist, the ingenious, the editor, the statesman, the erudite . . . they are not unappreciated . . . they fall in their place and do their work. The soul of the nation also does its work. No disguise can pass on it . . . no disguise can conceal from it. It rejects none, it permits all. Only toward as good as itself and toward the like of itself will it advance half-way. An individual is as superb as a nation when he has the qualities which make a superb nation. The soul of the largest and wealthiest and proudest nation may well go half-way to meet that of its poets. The signs are effectual. There is no fear of mistake. If the one is true the other is true. The proof of a poet is that his country absorbs him as affectionately as he has absorbed it.

LEAVES OF GRASS

[*Song of Myself*]

[1]

I CELEBRATE MYSELF,
And what I assume you shall assume,
For every atom belonging to me as good belongs to you.

I loafe and invite my soul,
I lean and loafe at my ease . . . . observing a spear of summer grass.   5

[2]

Houses and rooms are full of perfumes . . . . the shelves are crowded
    with perfumes,
I breathe the fragrance myself, and know it and like it,
The distillation would intoxicate me also, but I shall not let it.

The atmosphere is not a perfume . . . . it has no taste of the
    distillation . . . . it is odorless,
It is for my mouth forever . . . . I am in love with it,   10
I will go to the bank by the wood and become undisguised and naked,
I am mad for it to be in contact with me.

The smoke of my own breath,
Echoes, ripples, and buzzed whispers . . . . loveroot, silkthread,
    crotch and vine,
My respiration and inspiration . . . . the beating of my heart . . . .
    the passing of blood and air through my lungs,   15
The sniff of green leaves and dry leaves, and of the shore and
    darkcolored sea-rocks, and of hay in the barn,
The sound of the belched words of my voice . . . . words loosed to
    the eddies of the wind,

A few light kisses . . . . a few embraces . . . . a reaching around of arms,
The play of shine and shade on the trees as the supple boughs wag,
The delight alone or in the rush of the streets, or along the fields
    and hillsides,   20
The feeling of health . . . . the full-noon trill . . . . the song of me
    rising from bed and meeting the sun.

Have you reckoned a thousand acres much? Have you reckoned the
    earth much?
Have you practiced so long to learn to read?
Have you felt so proud to get at the meaning of poems?

Stop this day and night with me and you shall possess the origin of
    all poems,   25
You shall possess the good of the earth and sun . . . . there are millions
    of suns left,
You shall no longer take things at second or third hand . . . . nor look
    through the eyes of the dead . . . . nor feed on the spectres in
    books,
You shall not look through my eyes either, nor take things from me,
You shall listen to all sides and filter them from yourself.

[3]
I have heard what the talkers were talking . . . . the talk of the
    beginning and the end,   30
But I do not talk of the beginning or the end.

There was never any more inception than there is now,
Nor any more youth or age than there is now;
And will never be any more perfection than there is now,
Nor any more heaven or hell than there is now.   35

Urge and urge and urge,
Always the procreant urge of the world.

Out of the dimness opposite equals advance . . . . Always substance
    and increase,

Always a knit of identity . . . . always distinction . . . . always a breed
of life.

To elaborate is no avail . . . . Learned and unlearned feel that it   40
is so.

Sure as the most certain sure . . . . plumb in the uprights, well
entretied, braced in the beams,
Stout as a horse, affectionate, haughty, electrical,
I and this mystery here we stand.

Clear and sweet is my soul . . . . and clear and sweet is all that is not
my soul.

Lack one lacks both . . . . and the unseen is proved by the seen,   45
Till that becomes unseen and receives proof in its turn.

Showing the best and dividing it from the worst, age vexes age,
Knowing the perfect fitness and equanimity of things, while they
discuss I am silent, and go bathe and admire myself.

Welcome is every organ and attribute of me, and of any man hearty
and clean,
Not an inch nor a particle of an inch is vile, and none shall be less
familiar than the rest.   50

I am satisfied . . . . I see, dance, laugh, sing;
As God comes a loving bedfellow and sleeps at my side all night and
close on the peep of the day,
And leaves for me baskets covered with white towels bulging the house
with their plenty,
Shall I postpone my acceptation and realization and scream at my
eyes,
That they turn from gazing after and down the road,   55
And forthwith cipher and show me to a cent,
Exactly the contents of one, and exactly the contents of two, and
which is ahead?

[4]

Trippers and askers surround me,
People I meet . . . . the effect upon me of my early life . . . . of the
    ward and city I live in . . . . of the nation,
The latest news . . . . discoveries, inventions, societies . . . . authors
    old and new,   60
My dinner, dress, associates, looks, business, compliments, dues,
The real or fancied indifference of some man or woman I love,
The sickness of one of my folks—or of myself . . . . or ill-doing . . . .
    or loss or lack of money . . . . or depressions or exaltations,
They come to me days and nights and go from me again,
But they are not the Me myself.   65

Apart from the pulling and hauling stands what I am,
Stands amused, complacent, compassionating, idle, unitary,
Looks down, is erect, bends an arm on an impalpable certain rest,
Looks with its sidecurved head curious what will come next,
Both in and out of the game, and watching and wondering at it.   70

Backward I see in my own days where I sweated through fog with
    linguists and contenders,
I have no mockings or arguments . . . . I witness and wait.

[5]

I believe in you my soul . . . . the other I am must not abase itself
    to you,
And you must not be abased to the other.

Loafe with me on the grass . . . . loose the stop from your throat,   75
Not words, not music or rhyme I want . . . . not custom or lecture,
    not even the best,
Only the lull I like, the hum of your valved voice.

I mind how we lay in June, such a transparent summer morning;
You settled your head athwart my hips and gently turned over
    upon me,

And parted the shirt from my bosom-bone, and plunged your tongue
    to my barestript heart,   80
And reached till you felt my beard, and reached till you held my feet.

Swiftly arose and spread around me the peace and joy and knowl-
    edge that pass all the art and argument of the earth;
And I know that the hand of God is the elderhand of my own,
And I know that the spirit of God is the eldest brother of my own,
And that all the men ever born are also my brothers . . . . and the
    women my sisters and lovers,   85
And that a kelson of the creation is love;
And limitless are leaves stiff or drooping in the fields,
And brown ants in the little wells beneath them,
And mossy scabs of the wormfence, and heaped stones, and elder
    and mullen and pokeweed.

[6]

A child said, What is the grass? fetching it to me with full hands;   90
How could I answer the child? . . . . I do not know what it is any
    more than he.

I guess it must be the flag of my disposition, out of hopeful green stuff
    woven.

Or I guess it is the handkerchief of the Lord,
A scented gift and remembrancer designedly dropped,
Bearing the owner's name someway in the corners, that we may see
    and remark, and say Whose?   95

Or I guess the grass is itself a child . . . . the produced babe of the
    vegetation.

Or I guess it is a uniform hieroglyphic,
And it means, Sprouting alike in broad zones and narrow zones,
Growing among black folks as among white,
Kanuck, Tuckahoe, Congressman, Cuff, I give them the same, I
    receive them the same.   100

And now it seems to me the beautiful uncut hair of graves.

Tenderly will I use you curling grass,
It may be you transpire from the breasts of young men,
It may be if I had known them I would have loved them;
It may be you are from old people and from women, and from
    offspring taken soon out of their mothers' laps,   105
And here you are the mothers' laps.

This grass is very dark to be from the white heads of old mothers,
Darker than the colorless beards of old men,
Dark to come from under the faint red roofs of mouths.

O I perceive after all so many uttering tongues!   110
And I perceive they do not come from the roofs of mouths for
    nothing.

I wish I could translate the hints about the dead young men and
    women,
And the hints about old men and mothers, and the offspring taken
    soon out of their laps.

What do you think has become of the young and old men?
And what do you think has become of the women and children?   115

They are alive and well somewhere;
The smallest sprout shows there is really no death,
And if ever there was it led forward life, and does not wait at the
    end to arrest it,
And ceased the moment life appeared.

All goes onward and outward . . . . and nothing collapses,   120
And to die is different from what any one supposed, and luckier.

[7]

Has any one supposed it lucky to be born?
I hasten to inform him or her it is just as lucky to die, and I know it.

I pass death with the dying, and birth with the new-washed babe
    . . . . and am not contained between my hat and boots,
And peruse manifold objects, no two alike, and every one good,   125
The earth good, and the stars good, and their adjuncts all good.

I am not an earth nor an adjunct of an earth,
I am the mate and companion of people, all just as immortal and
    fathomless as myself;
They do not know how immortal, but I know.

Every kind for itself and its own . . . . for me mine male and female,   130
For me all that have been boys and that love women,
For me the man that is proud and feels how it stings to be slighted,
For me the sweetheart and the old maid . . . . for me mothers and
    the mothers of mothers,
For me lips that have smiled, eyes that have shed tears,
For me children and the begetters of children.   135

Who need be afraid of the merge?
Undrape . . . . you are not guilty to me, nor stale nor discarded,
I see through the broadcloth and gingham whether or no,
And am around, tenacious, acquisitive, tireless . . . . and can never
    be shaken away.

[8]

The little one sleeps in its cradle,   140
I lift the gauze and look a long time, and silently brush away flies
    with my hand.

The youngster and the redfaced girl turn aside up the bushy hill,
I peeringly view them from the top.

The suicide sprawls on the bloody floor of the bedroom,
It is so . . . . I witnessed the corpse . . . . there the pistol had fallen.   145

The blab of the pave . . . . the tires of carts and sluff of bootsoles
    and talk of the promenaders,

The heavy omnibus, the driver with his interrogating thumb, the
    clank of the shod horses on the granite floor,
The carnival of sleighs, the clinking and shouted jokes and pelts of
    snowballs;
The hurrahs for popular favorites . . . . the fury of roused mobs,
The flap of the curtained litter—the sick man inside, borne to the
    hospital,   150
The meeting of enemies, the sudden oath, the blows and fall,
The excited crowd—the policeman with his star quickly working his
    passage to the centre of the crowd;
The impressive stones that receive and return so many echoes,
The souls moving along . . . . are they invisible while the least atom
    of the stones is visible?
What groans of overfed or half-starved who fall on the flags
    sunstruck or in fits,   155
What exclamations of women taken suddenly, who hurry home and
    give birth to babes,
What living and buried speech is always vibrating here . . . . what
    howls restrained by decorum,
Arrests of criminals, slights, adulterous offers made, acceptances,
    rejections with convex lips,
I mind them or the resonance of them . . . . I come again and again.

[9]

The big doors of the country-barn stand open and ready,   160
The dried grass of the harvest-time loads the slow-drawn wagon,
The clear light plays on the brown gray and green intertinged,
The armfuls are packed to the sagging mow:
I am there . . . . I help . . . . I came stretched atop of the load,
I felt its soft jolts . . . . one leg reclined on the other,   165
I jump from the crossbeams, and seize the clover and timothy,
And roll head over heels, and tangle my hair full of wisps.

[10]

Alone far in the wilds and mountains I hunt,
Wandering amazed at my own lightness and glee,
In the late afternoon choosing a safe spot to pass the night,   170

Kindling a fire and broiling the freshkilled game,
Soundly falling asleep on the gathered leaves, my dog and gun by
    my side.

The Yankee clipper is under her three skysails . . . . she cuts the
    sparkle and scud,
My eyes settle the land . . . . I bend at her prow or shout joyously
    from the deck.

The boatmen and clamdiggers arose early and stopped for me,   175
I tucked my trowser-ends in my boots and went and had a good time,
You should have been with us that day round the chowder-kettle.

I saw the marriage of the trapper in the open air in the far-west . . . .
    the bride was a red girl,
Her father and his friends sat near by crosslegged and dumbly
    smoking . . . . they had moccasins to their feet and large thick
    blankets hanging from their shoulders;
On a bank lounged the trapper . . . . he was dressed mostly in skins
    . . . . his luxuriant beard and curls protected his neck,   180
One hand rested on his rifle . . . . the other hand held firmly the wrist
    of the red girl,
She had long eyelashes . . . . her head was bare . . . . her coarse straight
    locks descended upon her voluptuous limbs and reached to her
    feet.

The runaway slave came to my house and stopped outside,
I heard his motions crackling the twigs of the woodpile,
Through the swung half-door of the kitchen I saw him limpsey and
    weak,   185
And went where he sat on a log, and led him in and assured him,
And brought water and filled a tub for his sweated body and
    bruised feet,
And gave him a room that entered from my own, and gave him
    some coarse clean clothes,
And remember perfectly well his revolving eyes and his awkwardness,
And remember putting plasters on the galls of his neck and ankles;   190

He staid with me a week before he was recuperated and passed north,
I had him sit next me at table . . . . my firelock leaned in the corner.

[11]

Twenty-eight young men bathe by the shore,
Twenty-eight young men, and all so friendly,
Twenty-eight years of womanly life, and all so lonesome.   195

She owns the fine house by the rise of the bank,
She hides handsome and richly drest aft the blinds of the window.

Which of the young men does she like the best?
Ah the homeliest of them is beautiful to her.

Where are you off to, lady? for I see you,   200
You splash in the water there, yet stay stock still in your room.

Dancing and laughing along the beach came the twenty-ninth bather,
The rest did not see her, but she saw them and loved them.

The beards of the young men glistened with wet, it ran from their
    long hair,
Little streams passed all over their bodies.   205

An unseen hand also passed over their bodies,
It descended tremblingly from their temples and ribs.

The young men float on their backs, their white bellies swell to the
    sun . . . . they do not ask who seizes fast to them,
They do not know who puffs and declines with pendant and
    bending arch,
They do not think whom they souse with spray.   210

[12]

The butcher-boy puts off his killing-clothes, or sharpens his knife at
    the stall in the market,
I loiter enjoying his repartee and his shuffle and breakdown.

Blacksmiths with grimed and hairy chests environ the anvil,
Each has his main-sledge . . . . they are all out . . . . there is a great
    heat in the fire.

From the cinder-strewed threshold I follow their movements,   215
The lithe sheer of their waists plays even with their massive arms,
Overhand the hammers roll—overhand so slow—overhand so sure,
They do not hasten, each man hits in his place.

[13]

The negro holds firmly the reins of his four horses . . . . the block
    swags underneath on its tied-over chain,
The negro that drives the huge dray of the stoneyard . . . . steady
    and tall he stands poised on one leg on the stringpiece,   220
His blue shirt exposes his ample neck and breast and loosens over
    his hipband,
His glance is calm and commanding . . . . he tosses the slouch of his
    hat away from his forehead,
The sun falls on his crispy hair and moustache . . . . falls on the
    black of his polish'd and perfect limbs.

I behold the picturesque giant and love him . . . . and I do not stop
    there,
I go with the team also.   225

In me the caresser of life wherever moving . . . . backward as well
    as forward slueing,
To niches aside and junior bending.

Oxen that rattle the yoke or halt in the shade, what is that you
    express in your eyes?
It seems to me more than all the print I have read in my life.

My tread scares the wood-drake and wood-duck on my distant and
    daylong ramble,   230
They rise together, they slowly circle around.
. . . . I believe in those winged purposes,

And acknowledge the red yellow and white playing within me,
And consider the green and violet and the tufted crown intentional;
And do not call the tortoise unworthy because she is not something
　　else,　　　　　　　　　　　　　　　　　　　　　　　　235
And the mocking bird in the swamp never studied the gamut, yet
　　trills pretty well to me,
And the look of the bay mare shames silliness out of me.

[14]

The wild gander leads his flock through the cool night,
Ya-honk! he says, and sounds it down to me like an invitation;
The pert may suppose it meaningless, but I listen closer,
I find its purpose and place up there toward the November sky.　240

The sharphoofed moose of the north, the cat on the housesill, the
　　chickadee, the prairie-dog,
The litter of the grunting sow as they tug at her teats,
The brood of the turkeyhen, and she with her halfspread wings,
I see in them and myself the same old law.　　　　　　　　245

The press of my foot to the earth springs a hundred affections,
They scorn the best I can do to relate them.

I am enamoured of growing outdoors,
Of men that live among cattle or taste of the ocean or woods,
Of the builders and steerers of ships, of the wielders of axes and
　　mauls, of the drivers of horses,　　　　　　　　　　　　250
I can eat and sleep with them week in and week out.

What is commonest and cheapest and nearest and easiest is Me,
Me going in for my chances, spending for vast returns,
Adorning myself to bestow myself on the first that will take me,
Not asking the sky to come down to my goodwill,　　　　　255
Scattering it freely forever.

[15]

The pure contralto sings in the organloft,

The carpenter dresses his plank . . . . the tongue of his foreplane
    whistles its wild ascending lisp,

The married and unmarried children ride home to their thanks-
    giving dinner,

The pilot seizes the king-pin, he heaves down with a strong arm,   260

The mate stands braced in the whaleboat, lance and harpoon are
    ready,

The duck-shooter walks by silent and cautious stretches,

The deacons are ordained with crossed hands at the altar,

The spinning-girl retreats and advances to the hum of the big wheel,

The farmer stops by the bars of a Sunday and looks at the oats and
    rye,   265

The lunatic is carried at last to the asylum a confirmed case,

He will never sleep any more as he did in the cot in his mother's
    bedroom;

The jour printer with gray head and gaunt jaws works at his case,

He turns his quid of tobacco, his eyes get blurred with the manuscript;

The malformed limbs are tied to the anatomist's table,   270

What is removed drops horribly in a pail;

The quadroon girl is sold at the stand . . . . the drunkard nods by the
    barroom stove,

The machinist rolls up his sleeves . . . . the policeman travels his
    beat . . . . the gatekeeper marks who pass,

The young fellow drives the express-wagon . . . . I love him though I
    do not know him;

The half-breed straps on his light boots to compete in the race,   275

The western turkey-shooting draws old and young . . . . some lean on
    their rifles, some sit on logs,

Out from the crowd steps the marksman and takes his position and
    levels his piece;

The groups of newly-come immigrants cover the wharf or levee,

The woollypates hoe in the sugarfield, the overseer views them from
    his saddle;

The bugle calls in the ballroom, the gentlemen run for their partners,
    the dancers bow to each other;   280

The youth lies awake in the cedar-roofed garret and harks to the
    musical rain,

The Wolverine sets traps on the creek that helps fill the Huron,

The reformer ascends the platform, he spouts with his mouth and
    nose,

The company returns from its excursion, the darkey brings up the
    rear and bears the well-riddled target,

The squaw wrapt in her yellow-hemmed cloth is offering moccasins
    and beadbags for sale,   285

The connoisseur peers along the exhibition-gallery with halfshut eyes
    bent sideways,

The deckhands make fast the steamboat, the plank is thrown for the
    shoregoing passengers,

The young sister holds out the skein, the elder sister winds it off in a
    ball and stops now and then for the knots,

The one-year wife is recovering and happy, a week ago she bore her
    first child,

The cleanhaired Yankee girl works with her sewing-machine or in
    the factory or mill,   290

The nine months' gone is in the parturition chamber, her faintness
    and pains are advancing;

The pavingman leans on his twohanded rammer—the reporter's
    lead flies swiftly over the notebook—the signpainter is lettering
    with red and gold,

The canal-boy trots on the towpath—the bookkeeper counts at his
    desk—the shoemaker waxes his thread,

The conductor beats time for the band and all the performers
    follow him,

The child is baptised—the convert is making the first professions,   295

The regatta is spread on the bay . . . . how the white sails sparkle!

The drover watches his drove, he sings out to them that would stray,

The pedlar sweats with his pack on his back—the purchaser higgles
    about the odd cent,

The camera and plate are prepared, the lady must sit for her
    daguerreotype,

The bride unrumples her white dress, the minutehand of the clock
    moves slowly,   300

The opium eater reclines with rigid head and just-opened lips,

The prostitute draggles her shawl, her bonnet bobs on her tipsy and
pimpled neck,

The crowd laugh at her blackguard oaths, the men jeer and wink
to each other,

(Miserable! I do not laugh at your oaths nor jeer you,)

The President holds a cabinet council, he is surrounded by the
great secretaries,   305

On the piazza walk five friendly matrons with twined arms;

The crew of the fish-smack pack repeated layers of halibut in the
hold,

The Missourian crosses the plains toting his wares and his cattle,

The fare-collector goes through the train—he gives notice by the
jingling of loose change,

The floormen are laying the floor—the tinners are tinning the roof—
the masons are calling for mortar,   310

In single file each shouldering his hod pass onward the laborers;

Seasons pursuing each other the indescribable crowd is gathered . . . .
it is the Fourth of July . . . . what salutes of cannon and small
arms!

Seasons pursuing each other the plougher ploughs and the mower
mows and the wintergrain falls in the ground;

Off on the lakes the pikefisher watches and waits by the hole in the
frozen surface,

The stumps stand thick round the clearing, the squatter strikes deep
with his axe,   315

The flatboatmen make fast toward dusk near the cottonwood or
pekantrees,

The coon-seekers go now through the regions of the Red river, or
through those drained by the Tennessee, or through those of
the Arkansas,

The torches shine in the dark that hangs on the Chattahoochee or
Altamahaw;

Patriarchs sit at supper with sons and grandsons and great grandsons
around them,

In walls of adobie, in canvas tents, rest hunters and trappers after
their day's sport.   320

The city sleeps and the country sleeps,
The living sleep for their time . . . . the dead sleep for their time,
The old husband sleeps by his wife and the young husband sleeps
    by his wife;
And these one and all tend inward to me, and I tend outward to
    them,
And such as it is to be of these more or less I am.   325

[16]

I am of old and young, of the foolish as much as the wise,
Regardless of others, ever regardful of others,
Maternal as well as paternal, a child as well as a man,
Stuffed with the stuff that is coarse, and stuffed with the stuff that
    is fine,
One of the great nations, the nation of many nations—the smallest
    the same and the largest the same,   330
A southerner soon as a northerner, a planter nonchalant and
    hospitable,
A Yankee bound my own way . . . . ready for trade . . . . my joints
    the limberest joints on earth and the sternest joints on earth,
A Kentuckian walking the vale of the Elkhorn in my deerskin
    leggings,
A boatman over the lakes or bays or along coasts . . . . a Hoosier, a
    Badger, a Buckeye,
A Louisianian or Georgian, a poke-easy from sandhills and pines,   335
At home on Canadian snowshoes or up in the bush, or with fisher-
    men off Newfoundland,
At home in the fleet of iceboats, sailing with the rest and tacking,
At home on the hills of Vermont or in the woods of Maine or the
    Texan ranch,
Comrade of Californians . . . . comrade of free northwesterners,
    loving their big proportions,
Comrade of raftsmen and coalmen—comrade of all who shake hands
    and welcome to drink and meat;   340
A learner with the simplest, a teacher of the thoughtfulest,
A novice beginning experient of myriads of seasons,
Of every hue and trade and rank, of every caste and religion,

Not merely of the New World but of Africa Europe or Asia . . . . a
    wandering savage,
A farmer, mechanic, or artist . . . . a gentleman, sailor, lover or quaker, 345
A prisoner, fancy-man, rowdy, lawyer, physician or priest.

I resist anything better than my own diversity,
And breathe the air and leave plenty after me,
And am not stuck up, and am in my place.

The moth and the fisheggs are in their place,   350
The suns I see and the suns I cannot see are in their place,
The palpable is in its place and the impalpable is in its place.

[17]
These are the thoughts of all men in all ages and lands, they are not
    original with me,
If they are not yours as much as mine they are nothing or next to
    nothing,
If they do not enclose everything they are next to nothing,   355
If they are not the riddle and the untying of the riddle they are
    nothing,
If they are not just as close as they are distant they are nothing.

This is the grass that grows wherever the land is and the water is,
This is the common air that bathes the globe.

This is the breath of laws and songs and behaviour,   360
This is the tasteless water of souls . . . . this is the true sustenance,
It is for the illiterate . . . . it is for the judges of the supreme court . . . .
    it is for the federal capitol and the state capitols,
It is for the admirable communes of literary men and composers and
    singers and lecturers and engineers and savans,
It is for the endless races of working people and farmers and seamen.

[18]
This is the trill of a thousand clear cornets and scream of the octave
    flute and strike of triangles.   365

I play not a march for victors only . . . . I play great marches for
    conquered and slain persons.

Have you heard that it was good to gain the day?
I also say it is good to fall . . . . battles are lost in the same spirit in
    which they are won.

I sound triumphal drums for the dead . . . . I fling through my
    embouchures the loudest and gayest music to them,
Vivas to those who have failed, and to those whose war-vessels sank
    in the sea, and those themselves who sank in the sea,   370
And to all generals that lost engagements, and all overcome heroes,
    and the numberless unknown heroes equal to the greatest
    heroes known.

[19]

This is the meal pleasantly set . . . . this is the meat and drink for
    natural hunger,
It is for the wicked just the same as the righteous . . . . I make
    appointments with all,
I will not have a single person slighted or left away,
The keptwoman and sponger and thief are hereby invited . . . . the
    heavy-lipped slave is invited . . . . the venerealee is invited,   375
There shall be no difference between them and the rest.

This is the press of a bashful hand . . . . this is the float and odor of
    hair,
This is the touch of my lips to yours . . . . this is the murmur of
    yearning,
This is the far-off depth and height reflecting my own face,
This is the thoughtful merge of myself and the outlet again.   380

Do you guess I have some intricate purpose?
Well I have . . . . for the April rain has, and the mica on the side of
    a rock has.

Do you take it I would astonish?

Does the daylight astonish? or the early redstart twittering through
    the woods?
Do I astonish more than they? 385

This hour I tell things in confidence,
I might not tell everybody but I will tell you.

[20]

Who goes there! hankering, gross, mystical, nude?
How is it I extract strength from the beef I eat?

What is a man anyhow? What am I? and what are you? 390
All I mark as my own you shall offset it with your own,
Else it were time lost listening to me.

I do not snivel that snivel the world over,
That months are vacuums and the ground but wallow and filth,
That life is a suck and a sell, and nothing remains at the end but
    threadbare crape and tears. 395

Whimpering and truckling fold with powders for invalids . . . .
    conformity goes to the fourth-removed,
I cock my hat as I please indoors or out.

Shall I pray? Shall I venerate and be ceremonious?
I have pried through the strata and analyzed to a hair,
And counselled with doctors and calculated close and found no
    sweeter fat than sticks to my own bones. 400

In all people I see myself, none more and not one a barleycorn less,
And the good or bad I say of myself I say of them.

And I know I am solid and sound,
To me the converging objects of the universe perpetually flow,
All are written to me, and I must get what the writing means. 405

And I know I am deathless,

I know this orbit of mine cannot be swept by a carpenter's compass,
I know I shall not pass like a child's carlacue cut with a burnt stick
    at night.

I know I am august,
I do not trouble my spirit to vindicate itself or be understood,   410
I see that the elementary laws never apologize,
I reckon I behave no prouder than the level I plant my house by
    after all.

I exist as I am, that is enough,
If no other in the world be aware I sit content,
And if each and all be aware I sit content.   415

One world is aware, and by far the largest to me, and that is myself,
And whether I come to my own today or in ten thousand or ten
    million years,
I can cheerfully take it now, or with equal cheerfulness I can wait.

My foothold is tenoned and mortised in granite,
I laugh at what you call dissolution,   420
And I know the amplitude of time.

[21]

I am the poet of the body,
And I am the poet of the soul.

The pleasures of heaven are with me, and the pains of hell are with
    me,
The first I graft and increase upon myself . . . . the latter I translate
    into a new tongue.   425

I am the poet of the woman the same as the man,
And I say it is as great to be a woman as to be a man,
And I say there is nothing greater than the mother of men.

I chant a new chant of dilation or pride,

We have had ducking and deprecating about enough,   430
I show that size is only development.

Have you outstript the rest? Are you the President?
It is a trifle . . . . they will more than arrive there every one, and
    still pass on.

I am he that walks with the tender and growing night;
I call to the earth and sea half-held by the night.   435

Press close barebosomed night! Press close magnetic nourishing night!
Night of south winds! Night of the large few stars!
Still nodding night! Mad naked summer night!

Smile O voluptuous coolbreathed earth!
Earth of the slumbering and liquid trees!   440
Earth of departed sunset! Earth of the mountains misty-topt!
Earth of the vitreous pour of the full moon just tinged with blue!
Earth of shine and dark mottling the tide of the river!
Earth of the limpid gray of clouds brighter and clearer for my sake!
Far-swooping elbowed earth! Rich apple-blossomed earth!   445
Smile, for your lover comes!

Prodigal! you have given me love! . . . . therefore I to you give love!
O unspeakable passionate love!

Thruster holding me tight and that I hold tight!
We hurt each other as the bridegroom and the bride hurt each other. 450

[22]

You sea! I resign myself to you also . . . . I guess what you mean,
I behold from the beach your crooked inviting fingers,
I believe you refuse to go back without feeling of me;
We must have a turn together . . . . I undress . . . . hurry me out of
    sight of the land,
Cushion me soft . . . . rock me in billowy drowse,   455
Dash me with amorous wet . . . . I can repay you.

Sea of stretched ground-swells!
Sea breathing broad and convulsive breaths!
Sea of the brine of life! Sea of unshovelled and always-ready graves!
Howler and scooper of storms! Capricious and dainty sea!　　　460
I am integral with you . . . . I too am of one phase and of all phases.

Partaker of influx and efflux . . . . extoller of hate and conciliation,
Extoller of amies and those that sleep in each others' arms.

I am he attesting sympathy;
Shall I make my list of things in the house and skip the house that
　　　supports them?　　　465

I am the poet of commonsense and of the demonstrable and of
　　　immortality;
And am not the poet of goodness only . . . . I do not decline to be
　　　the poet of wickedness also.

Washes and razors for foofoos . . . . for me freckles and a bristling
　　　beard.

What blurt is it about virtue and about vice?
Evil propels me, and reform of evil propels me . . . . I stand
　　　indifferent,　　　470
My gait is no faultfinder's or rejecter's gait,
I moisten the roots of all that has grown.

Did you fear some scrofula out of the unflagging pregnancy?
Did you guess the celestial laws are yet to be worked over and
　　　rectified?

I step up to say that what we do is right and what we affirm is
　　　right . . . . and some is only the ore of right,　　　475
Witnesses of us . . . . one side a balance and the antipodal side a
　　　balance,
Soft doctrine as steady help as stable doctrine,
Thoughts and deeds of the present our rouse and early start.

This minute that comes to me over the past decillions,
There is no better than it and now.   480

What behaved well in the past or behaves well today is not such a
      wonder,
The wonder is always and always how there can be a mean man or
      an infidel.

[23]
Endless unfolding of words of ages!
And mine a word of the modern . . . . a word en masse.

A word of the faith that never balks,   485
One time as good as another time . . . . here or henceforward it is
      all the same to me.

A word of reality . . . . materialism first and last imbuing.

Hurrah for positive science! Long live exact demonstration!
Fetch stonecrop and mix it with cedar and branches of lilac;
This is the lexicographer or chemist . . . . this made a grammar of
      the old cartouches,   490
These mariners put the ship through dangerous unknown seas,
This is the geologist, and this works with the scalpel, and this is a
      mathematician.

Gentlemen I receive you, and attach and clasp hands with you,
The facts are useful and real . . . . they are not my dwelling I
      enter by them to an area of the dwelling.

I am less the reminder of property or qualities, and more the
      reminder of life,   495
And go on the square for my own sake and for other's sake,
And make short account of neuters and geldings, and favor men and
      women fully equipped,
And beat the gong of revolt, and stop with fugitives and them that
      plot and conspire.

[24]

Walt Whitman, an American, one of the roughs, a kosmos,
Disorderly fleshy and sensual . . . . eating drinking and breeding,   500
No sentimentalist . . . . no stander above men and women or apart
      from them . . . . no more modest than immodest.

Unscrew the locks from the doors!
Unscrew the doors themselves from their jambs!

Whoever degrades another degrades me . . . . and whatever is done or
      said returns at last to me,
And whatever I do or say I also return.   505

Through me the afflatus surging and surging . . . . through me the
      current and index.

I speak the password primeval . . . . I give the sign of democracy;
By God! I will accept nothing which all cannot have their counter-
      part of on the same terms.

Through me many long dumb voices,
Voices of the interminable generations of slaves,   510
Voices of prostitutes and of deformed persons,
Voices of the diseased and despairing, and of thieves and dwarfs,
Voices of cycles of preparation and accretion,
And of the threads that connect the stars—and of wombs, and of the
      fatherstuff,
And of the rights of them the others are down upon,   515
Of the trivial and flat and foolish and despised,
Of fog in the air and beetles rolling balls of dung.

Through me forbidden voices,
Voices of sexes and lusts . . . . voices veiled, and I remove the veil,
Voices indecent by me clarified and transfigured.   520

I do not press my finger across my mouth,
I keep as delicate around the bowels as around the head and heart,

Copulation is no more rank to me than death is.

I believe in the flesh and the appetites,
Seeing hearing and feeling are miracles, and each part and tag of
    me is a miracle.   525

Divine am I inside and out, and I make holy whatever I touch or
    am touched from;
The scent of these arm-pits is aroma finer than prayer,
This head is more than churches or bibles or creeds.

If I worship any particular thing it shall be some of the spread of my
    body;   530
Translucent mould of me it shall be you,
Shaded ledges and rests, firm masculine coulter, it shall be you,
Whatever goes to the tilth of me it shall be you,
You my rich blood, your milky stream pale strippings of my life;
Breast that presses against other breasts it shall be you,
My brain it shall be your occult convolutions,   535
Root of washed sweet-flag, timorous pond-snipe, nest of guarded
    duplicate eggs, it shall be you,
Mixed tussled hay of head and beard and brawn it shall be you,
Trickling sap of maple, fibre of manly wheat, it shall be you;
Sun so generous it shall be you,
Vapors lighting and shading my face it shall be you,   540
You sweaty brooks and dews it shall be you,
Winds whose soft-tickling genitals rub against me it shall be you,
Broad muscular fields, branches of liveoak, loving lounger in my
    winding paths, it shall be you,
Hands I have taken, face I have kissed, mortal I have ever touched,
    it shall be you.

I dote on myself . . . . there is that lot of me, and all so luscious,   545
Each moment and whatever happens thrills me with joy.

I cannot tell how my ankles bend . . . . nor whence the cause of my
    faintest wish,

Nor the cause of the friendship I emit . . . . nor the cause of the
    friendship I take again.

To walk up my stoop is unaccountable . . . . I pause to consider if it
    really be,
That I eat and drink is spectacle enough for the great authors and
    schools,   550
A morning-glory at my window satisfies me more than the
    metaphysics of books.

To behold the daybreak!
The little light fades the immense and diaphanous shadows,
The air tastes good to my palate.

Hefts of the moving world at innocent gambols, silently rising,
    freshly exuding,   555
Scooting obliquely high and low.

Something I cannot see puts upward libidinous prongs,
Seas of bright juice suffuse heaven.

The earth by the sky staid with . . . . the daily close of their junction,
The heaved challenge from the east that moment over my head,   560
The mocking taunt, See then whether you shall be master!

[25]
Dazzling and tremendous how quick the sunrise would kill me,
If I could not now and always send sunrise out of me.

We also ascend dazzling and tremendous as the sun,
We found our own my soul in the calm and cool of the daybreak.   565

My voice goes after what my eyes cannot reach,
With the twirl of my tongue I encompass worlds and volumes of
    worlds.

Speech is the twin of my vision . . . . it is unequal to measure itself.

It provokes me forever,
It says sarcastically, Walt, you understand enough . . . . why don't
    you let it out then? 570

Come now I will not be tantalized . . . . you conceive too much of
    articulation.

Do you not know how the buds beneath are folded?
Waiting in gloom protected by frost,
The dirt receding before my prophetical screams,
I underlying causes to balance them at last, 575
My knowledge my live parts . . . . it keeping tally with the meaning
    of things,
Happiness . . . . which whoever hears me let him or her set out in
    search of this day.

My final merit I refuse you . . . . I refuse putting from me the best
    I am.

Encompass worlds but never try to encompass me,
I crowd your noisiest talk by looking toward you. 580

Writing and talk do not prove me,
I carry the plenum of proof and every thing else in my face,
With the hush of my lips I confound the topmost skeptic.

[26]
I think I will do nothing for a long time but listen,
And accrue what I hear into myself . . . . and let sounds contribute
    toward me. 585

I hear the bravuras of birds . . . . the bustle of growing wheat . . . .
    gossip of flames . . . . clack of sticks cooking my meals.

I hear the sound of the human voice . . . . a sound I love,
I hear all sounds as they are tuned to their uses . . . . sounds of the
    city and sounds out of the city . . . . sounds of the day and night;

Talkative young ones to those that like them . . . . the recitative of
    fish-pedlars and fruit-pedlars . . . . the loud laugh of workpeople
    at their meals,
The angry base of disjointed friendship . . . . the faint tones of
    the sick,   590
The judge with hands tight to the desk, his shaky lips pronouncing
    a death-sentence,
The heave'e'yo of stevedores unlading ships by the wharves . . . . the
    refrain of the anchor-lifters;
The ring of alarm-bells . . . . the cry of fire . . . . the whirr of swift-
    streaking engines and hose-carts with premonitory tinkles and
    colored lights,
The steam-whistle . . . . the solid roll of the train of approaching cars;
The slow-march played at night at the head of the association,   595
They go to guard some corpse . . . . the flag-tops are draped with
    black muslin.

I hear the violincello or man's heart complaint,
And hear the keyed cornet or else the echo of sunset.

I hear the chorus . . . . it is a grand-opera . . . . this indeed is music!

A tenor large and fresh as the creation fills me,   600
The orbic flex of his mouth is pouring and filling me full.

I hear the trained soprano . . . . she convulses me like the climax of
    my love-grip;
The orchestra whirls me wider than Uranus flies,
It wrenches unnamable ardors from my breast,
It throbs me to gulps of the farthest down horror,   605
It sails me . . . . I dab with bare feet . . . . they are licked by the
    indolent waves,
I am exposed . . . . cut by bitter and poisoned hail,
Steeped amid honeyed morphine . . . . my windpipe squeezed in the
    fakes of death,
Let up again to feel the puzzle of puzzles,
And that we call Being.   610

[27]

To be in any form, what is that?
If nothing lay more developed the quahaug and its callous shell
    were enough.

Mine is no callous shell,
I have instant conductors all over me whether I pass or stop,
They seize every object and lead it harmlessly through me.   615

I merely stir, press, feel with my fingers, and am happy,
To touch my person to some one else's is about as much as I can
    stand.

[28]

Is this then a touch? . . . . quivering me to a new identity,
Flames and ether making a rush for my veins,
Treacherous tip of me reaching and crowding to help them,   620
My flesh and blood playing out lightning, to strike what is hardly
    different from myself,
On all sides prurient provokers stiffening my limbs,
Straining the udder of my heart for its withheld drip,
Behaving licentious toward me, taking no denial,
Depriving me of my best as for a purpose,   625
Unbuttoning my clothes and holding me by the bare waist,
Deluding my confusion with the calm of the sunlight and pasture
    fields,
Immodestly sliding the fellow-senses away,
They bribed to swap off with touch, and go and graze at the edges
    of me,
No consideration, no regard for my draining strength or my anger,   630
Fetching the rest of the herd around to enjoy them awhile,
Then all uniting to stand on a headland and worry me.

The sentries desert every other part of me,
They have left me helpless to a red marauder,
They all come to the headland to witness and assist against me.   635

I am given up by traitors;
I talk wildly . . . . I have lost my wits . . . . I and nobody else am the
　　greatest traitor,
I went myself first to the headland . . . . my own hands carried me
　　there.

You villain touch! what are you doing? . . . . my breath is tight in
　　its throat;
Unclench your floodgates! you are too much for me.　　　　　　640

[29]

Blind loving wrestling touch! Sheathed hooded sharptoothed touch!
Did it make you ache so leaving me?

Parting tracked by arriving . . . . perpetual payment of the perpetual
　　loan,
Rich showering rain, and recompense richer afterward.

Sprouts take and accumulate . . . . stand by the curb prolific and vital,　645
Landscapes projected masculine full-sized and golden.

[30]

All truths wait in all things,
They neither hasten their own delivery nor resist it,
They do not need the obstetric forceps of the surgeon,
The insignificant is as big to me as any,　　　　　　　　　　650
What is less or more than a touch?

Logic and sermons never convince,
The damp of the night drives deeper into my soul.

Only what proves itself to every man and woman is so,
Only what nobody denies is so.　　　　　　　　　　　　655

A minute and a drop of me settle my brain;
I believe the soggy clods shall become lovers and lamps,
And a compend of compends is the meat of a man or woman,

And a summit and flower there is the feeling they have for each other,
And they are to branch boundlessly out of that lesson until it
    becomes omnific, 660
And until every one shall delight us, and we them.

[31]

I believe a leaf of grass is no less than the journeywork of the stars,
And the pismire is equally perfect, and a grain of sand, and the egg
    of the wren,
And the tree-toad is a chef-d'œuvre for the highest,
And the running blackberry would adorn the parlors of heaven, 665
And the narrowest hinge in my hand puts to scorn all machinery,
And the cow crunching with depressed head surpasses any statue,
And a mouse is miracle enough to stagger sextillions of infidels,
And I could come every afternoon of my life to look at the farmer's
    girl boiling her iron tea-kettle and baking shortcake.

I find I incorporate gneiss and coal and long-threaded moss and
    fruits and grains and esculent roots, 670
And am stucco'd with quadrupeds and birds all over,
And have distanced what is behind me for good reasons,
And call any thing close again when I desire it.

In vain the speeding or shyness,
In vain the plutonic rocks send their old heat against my approach,
In vain the mastodon retreats beneath its own powdered bones, 675
In vain objects stand leagues off and assume manifold shapes,
In vain the ocean settling in hollows and the great monsters lying low,
In vain the buzzard houses herself with the sky,
In vain the snake slides through the creepers and logs, 680
In vain the elk takes to the inner passes of the woods,
In vain the razorbilled auk sails far north to Labrador,
I follow quickly . . . . I ascend to the nest in the fissure of the cliff.

[32]

I think I could turn and live awhile with the animals . . . . they are
    so placid and self-contained,

I stand and look at them sometimes half the day long.   685

They do not sweat and whine about their condition,
They do not lie awake in the dark and weep for their sins,
They do not make me sick discussing their duty to God,
Not one is dissatisfied . . . . not one is demented with the mania of
    owning things,
Not one kneels to another nor to his kind that lived thousands of
    years ago,   690
Not one is respectable or industrious over the whole earth.

So they show their relations to me and I accept them;
They bring me tokens of myself . . . . they evince them plainly in
    their possession.

I do not know where they got those tokens,
I must have passed that way untold times ago and negligently dropt
    them,   695
Myself moving forward then and now and forever,
Gathering and showing more always and with velocity,
Infinite and omnigenous and the like of these among them;
Not too exclusive toward the reachers of my remembrancers,
Picking out here one that shall be my amie,   700
Choosing to go with him on brotherly terms.

A gigantic beauty of a stallion, fresh and responsive to my caresses,
Head high in the forehead and wide between the ears,
Limbs glossy and supple, tail dusting the ground,
Eyes well apart and full of sparkling wickedness . . . . ears finely cut
    and flexibly moving.   705

His nostrils dilate . . . . my heels embrace him . . . . his well built limbs
    tremble with pleasure . . . . we speed around and return.

I but use you a moment and then I resign you stallion . . . . and do
    not need your paces, and outgallop them,
And myself as I stand or sit pass faster than you.

[33]

Swift wind! Space! My Soul! Now I know it is true what I guessed
    at;
What I guessed when I loafed on the grass,   710
What I guessed while I lay alone in my bed . . . . and again as I
    walked the beach under the paling stars of the morning.

My ties and ballasts leave me . . . . I travel . . . . I sail . . . . my
    elbows rest in the sea-gaps,
I skirt the sierras . . . . my palms cover continents,
I am afoot with my vision.

By the city's quadrangular houses . . . . in log-huts, or camping
    with lumbermen,   715
Along the ruts of the turnpike . . . . along the dry gulch and rivulet bed,
Hoeing my onion-patch, and rows of carrots and parsnips . . . .
    crossing savannas . . . . trailing in forests,
Prospecting . . . . gold-digging . . . . girdling the trees of a new
    purchase,
Scorched ankle-deep by the hot sand . . . . hauling my boat down
    the shallow river;
Where the panther walks to and fro on a limb overhead . . . . where
    the buck turns furiously at the hunter,   720
Where the rattlesnake suns his flabby length on a rock . . . . where
    the otter is feeding on fish,
Where the alligator in his tough pimples sleeps by the bayou,
Where the black bear is searching for roots or honey . . . . where the
    beaver pats the mud with his paddle-tail;
Over the growing sugar . . . . over the cottonplant . . . . over the rice
    in its low moist field;
Over the sharp-peaked farmhouse with its scalloped scum and
    slender shoots from the gutters;   725
Over the western persimmon . . . . over the longleaved corn and the
    delicate blue-flowered flax;
Over the white and brown buckwheat, a hummer and a buzzer
    there with the rest,

Over the dusky green of the rye as it ripples and shades in the breeze;
Scaling mountains . . . . pulling myself cautiously up . . . . holding
    on by low scragged limbs,
Walking the path worn in the grass and beat through the leaves of
    the brush;   730
Where the quail is whistling betwixt the woods and the wheatlot,
Where the bat flies in the July eve . . . . where the great goldbug
    drops through the dark;
Where the flails keep time on the barn floor,
Where the brook puts out of the roots of the old tree and flows to
    the meadow,
Where cattle stand and shake away flies with the tremulous shud-
    dering of their hides,   735
Where the cheese-cloth hangs in the kitchen, and andirons straddle
    the hearth-slab, and cobwebs fall in festoons from the rafters;
Where triphammers crash . . . . where the press is whirling its
    cylinders;
Wherever the human heart beats with terrible throes out of its ribs;
Where the pear-shaped balloon is floating aloft . . . . floating in it
    myself and looking composedly down;
Where the life-car is drawn on the slipnoose . . . . where the heat
    hatches pale-green eggs in the dented sand,   740
Where the she-whale swims with her calves and never forsakes them,
Where the steamship trails hindways its long pennant of smoke,
Where the ground-shark's fin cuts like a black chip out of the water,
Where the half-burned brig is riding on unknown currents,
Where shells grow to her slimy deck, and the dead are corrupting
    below;   745
Where the striped and starred flag is borne at the head of the
    regiments;
Approaching Manhattan, up by the long-stretching island,
Under Niagara, the cataract falling like a veil over my countenance;
Upon a door-step . . . . upon the horse-block of hard wood outside,
Upon the race-course, or enjoying pic-nics or jigs or a good game
    of base-ball,   750
At he-festivals with blackguard jibes and ironical license and bull-
    dances and drinking and laughter,

At the cider-mill, tasting the sweet of the brown sqush . . . . sucking
 the juice through a straw,
At apple-peelings, wanting kisses for all the red fruit I find,
At musters and beach-parties and friendly bees and huskings and
 house-raisings;
Where the mockingbird sounds his delicious gurgles, and cackles and
 screams and weeps,   755
Where the hay-rick stands in the barnyard, and the dry-stalks are
 scattered, and the brood cow waits in the hovel,
Where the bull advances to do his masculine work, and the stud to
 the mare, and the cock is treading the hen,
Where the heifers browse, and the geese nip their food with short jerks;
Where the sundown shadows lengthen over the limitless and lone-
 some prairie,
Where the herds of buffalo make a crawling spread of the square
 miles far and near;   760
Where the hummingbird shimmers . . . . where the neck of the
 longlived swan is curving and winding;
Where the laughing-gull scoots by the slappy shore and laughs her
 near-human laugh;
Where beehives range on a gray bench in the garden half-hid by
 the high weeds;
Where the band-necked partridges roost in a ring on the ground
 with their heads out;
Where burial coaches enter the arched gates of a cemetery;   765
Where winter wolves bark amid wastes of snow and icicled trees;
Where the yellow-crowned heron comes to the edge of the marsh at
 night and feeds upon small crabs;
Where the splash of swimmers and divers cools the warm noon;
Where the katydid works her chromatic reed on the walnut-tree
 over the well;
Through patches of citrons and cucumbers with silver-wired leaves, 770
Through the salt-lick or orange glade . . . . or under conical firs;
Through the gymnasium . . . . through the curtained saloon . . . .
 through the office or public hall;
Pleased with the native and pleased with the foreign . . . . pleased
 with the new and old,

Pleased with women, the homely as well as the handsome,
Pleased with the quakeress as she puts off her bonnet and talks
    melodiously,   775
Pleased with the primitive tunes of the choir of the whitewashed
    church,
Pleased with the earnest words of the sweating Methodist preacher,
    or any preacher . . . . looking seriously at the camp-meeting;
Looking in at the shop-windows in Broadway the whole forenoon
    . . . . pressing the flesh of my nose to the thick plate-glass,
Wandering the same afternoon with my face turned up to the clouds;
My right and left arms round the sides of two friends and I in the
    middle;   780
Coming home with the bearded and dark-cheeked bush-boy . . . .
    riding behind him at the drape of the day;
Far from the settlements studying the print of animals' feet, or the
    moccasin print;
By the cot in the hospital reaching lemonade to a feverish patient,
By the coffined corpse when all is still, examining with a candle;
Voyaging to every port to dicker and adventure;   785
Hurrying with the modern crowd, as eager and fickle as any,
Hot toward one I hate, ready in my madness to knife him;
Solitary at midnight in my back yard, my thoughts gone from me a
    long while,
Walking the old hills of Judea with the beautiful gentle god by my
    side;
Speeding through space . . . . speeding through heaven and the stars, 790
Speeding amid the seven satellites and the broad ring and the
    diameter of eighty thousand miles,
Speeding with tailed meteors . . . . throwing fire-balls like the rest,
Carrying the crescent child that carries its own full mother in its
    belly:
Storming enjoying planning loving cautioning,
Backing and filling, appearing and disappearing,   795
I tread day and night such roads.

I visit the orchards of God and look at the spheric product,
And look at quintillions ripened, and look at quintillions green.

I fly the flight of the fluid and swallowing soul,
My course runs below the soundings of plummets. 800

I help myself to material and immaterial,
No guard can shut me off, no law can prevent me.

I anchor my ship for a little while only,
My messengers continually cruise away or bring their returns
    to me.

I go hunting polar furs and the seal . . . . leaping chasms with a
    pike-pointed staff . . . . clinging to topples of brittle and blue. 805

I ascend to the foretruck . . . . I take my place late at night in the
    crow's nest . . . . we sail through the arctic sea . . . . it is plenty
    light enough,
Through the clear atmosphere I stretch around on the wonderful
    beauty,
The enormous masses of ice pass me and I pass them . . . . the
    scenery is plain in all directions,
The white-topped mountains point up in the distance . . . . I fling
    out my fancies toward them;
We are about approaching some great battlefield in which we are
    soon to be engaged, 810
We pass the colossal outposts of the encampment . . . . we pass with
    still feet and caution;
Or we are entering by the suburbs some vast and ruined city . . . .
    the blocks and fallen architecture more than all the living cities
    of the globe.

I am a free companion . . . . I bivouac by invading watchfires.

I turn the bridegroom out of bed and stay with the bride myself,
And tighten her all night to my thighs and lips. 815

My voice is the wife's voice, the screech by the rail of the stairs,
They fetch my man's body up dripping and drowned.

I understand the large hearts of heroes,
The courage of present times and all times;
How the skipper saw the crowded and rudderless wreck of the
    steamship, and death chasing it up and down the storm,   820
How he knuckled tight and gave not back one inch, and was
    faithful of days and faithful of nights,
And chalked in large letters on a board, Be of good cheer, We will
    not desert you;
How he saved the drifting company at last,
How the lank loose-gowned women looked when boated from the
    side of their prepared graves,
How the silent old-faced infants, and the lifted sick, and the sharp-
    lipped unshaved men;   825
All this I swallow and it tastes good . . . . I like it well, and it
    becomes mine,
I am the man . . . . I suffered . . . . I was there.

The disdain and calmness of martyrs,
The mother condemned for a witch and burnt with dry wood, and
    her children gazing on;
The hounded slave that flags in the race and leans by the fence,
    blowing and covered with sweat,   830
The twinges that sting like needles his legs and neck,
The murderous buckshot and the bullets,
All these I feel or am.

I am the hounded slave . . . . I wince at the bite of the dogs,
Hell and despair are upon me . . . . crack and again crack the
    marksmen,   835
I clutch the rails of the fence . . . . my gore dribs thinned with the
    ooze of my skin,
I fall on the weeds and stones,
The riders spur their unwilling horses and haul close,
They taunt my dizzy ears . . . . they beat me violently over the head
    with their whip-stocks.

Agonies are one of my changes of garments;   840

I do not ask the wounded person how he feels . . . . I myself
    become the wounded person,
My hurt turns livid upon me as I lean on a cane and observe.

I am the mashed fireman with breastbone broken . . . . tumbling
    walls buried me in their debris,
Heat and smoke I inspired . . . . I heard the yelling shouts of my
    comrades,
I heard the distant click of their picks and shovels;   845
They have cleared the beams away . . . . they tenderly lift me forth.

I lie in the night air in my red shirt . . . . the pervading hush is for
    my sake,
Painless after all I lie, exhausted but not so unhappy,
White and beautiful are the faces around me . . . . the heads are
    bared of their fire-caps,
The kneeling crowd fades with the light of the torches.   850

Distant and dead resuscitate,
They show as the dial or move as the hands of me . . . . and I am
    the clock myself.

I am an old artillerist, and tell of some fort's bombardment . . . . and
    am there again.

Again the reveille of drummers . . . . again the attacking cannon and
    mortars and howitzers,
Again the attacked send their cannon responsive.   855

I take part . . . . I see and hear the whole,
The cries and curses and roar . . . . the plaudits for well aimed shots,
The ambulanza slowly passing and trailing its red drip,
Workmen searching after damages and to make indispensable
    repairs,
The fall of grenades through the rent roof . . . . the fan-shaped
    explosion,
The whizz of limbs heads stone wood and iron high in the air.   860

Again gurgles the mouth of my dying general . . . . he furiously waves
　　with his hand,
He gasps through the clot . . . . Mind not me . . . . mind . . . . the
　　entrenchments.

[34]

I tell not the fall of Alamo . . . . not one escaped to tell the fall of
　　Alamo,
The hundred and fifty are dumb yet at Alamo.　　　　　　　　　　865

Hear now the tale of a jetblack sunrise,
Hear of the murder in cold blood of four hundred and twelve young
　　men.

Retreating they had formed in a hollow square with their baggage
　　for breastworks,
Nine hundred lives out of the surrounding enemy's nine times their
　　number was the price they took in advance,
Their colonel was wounded and their ammunition gone,　　　　　870
They treated for an honorable capitulation, received writing and
　　seal, gave up their arms, and marched back prisoners of war.

They were the glory of the race of rangers,
Matchless with a horse, a rifle, a song, a supper or a courtship,
Large, turbulent, brave, handsome, generous, proud and affectionate,
Bearded, sunburnt, dressed in the free costume of hunters,　　　875
Not a single one over thirty years of age.

The second Sunday morning they were brought out in squads and
　　massacred . . . . it was beautiful early summer,
The work commenced about five o'clock and was over by eight.

None obeyed the command to kneel,
Some made a mad and helpless rush . . . . some stood stark and
　　straight,　　　　　　　　　　　　　　　　　　　　　　　　880
A few fell at once, shot in the temple or heart . . . . the living and
　　dead lay together,

The maimed and mangled dug in the dirt . . . . the new-comers saw
    them there;
Some half-killed attempted to crawl away,
These were dispatched with bayonets or battered with the blunts of
    muskets;
A youth not seventeen years old seized his assassin till two more
    came to release him,   885
The three were all torn, and covered with the boy's blood.

At eleven o'clock began the burning of the bodies;
And that is the tale of the murder of the four hundred and twelve
    young men,
And that was a jetblack sunrise.

[35]
Did you read in the seabooks of the oldfashioned frigate-fight?   890
Did you learn who won by the light of the moon and stars?

Our foe was no skulk in his ship, I tell you,
His was the English pluck, and there is no tougher or truer, and
    never was, and never will be;
Along the lowered eve he came, horribly raking us.

We closed with him . . . . the yards entangled . . . . the cannon
    touched,   895
My captain lashed fast with his own hands.

We had received some eighteen-pound shots under the water,
On our lower-gun-deck two large pieces had burst at the first fire,
    killing all around and blowing up overhead.

Ten o'clock at night, and the full moon shining and the leaks on the
    gain, and five feet of water reported,
The master-at-arms loosing the prisoners confined in the after-hold
    to give them a chance for themselves.   900

The transit to and from the magazine was now stopped by the sentinels,

They saw so many strange faces they did not know whom to trust.

Our frigate was afire . . . . the other asked if we demanded quarters?
    if our colors were struck and the fighting done?

I laughed content when I heard the voice of my little captain,
We have not struck, he composedly cried, We have just begun our
    part of the fighting.   905

Only three guns were in use,
One was directed by the captain himself against the enemy's
    mainmast,
Two well-served with grape and canister silenced his musketry and
    cleared his decks.

The tops alone seconded the fire of this little battery, especially the
    maintop,
They all held out bravely during the whole of the action.   910

Not a moment's cease,
The leaks gained fast on the pumps . . . . the fire eat toward the
    powder-magazine,
One of the pumps was shot away . . . . it was generally thought we
    were sinking.

Serene stood the little captain,
He was not hurried . . . . his voice was neither high nor low,   915
His eyes gave more light to us than our battle-lanterns.

Toward twelve at night, there in the beams of the moon they
    surrendered to us.

[36]
Stretched and still lay the midnight,
Two great hulls motionless on the breast of the darkness,
Our vessel riddled and slowly sinking . . . . preparations to pass to the
    one we had conquered,   920

The captain on the quarter deck coldly giving his orders through a
    countenance white as a sheet,
Near by the corpse of the child that served in the cabin,
The dead face of an old salt with long white hair and carefully
    curled whiskers,
The flames spite of all that could be done flickering aloft and
    below,
The husky voices of the two or three officers yet fit for duty,   925
Formless stacks of bodies and bodies by themselves . . . . dabs of flesh
    upon the masts and spars,
The cut of cordage and dangle of rigging . . . . the slight shock of the
    soothe of waves,
Black and impressive guns, and litter of powder-parcels, and the
    strong scent,
Delicate sniffs of the seabreeze . . . . smells of sedgy grass and fields
    by the shore . . . . death-messages given in charge to survivors,
The hiss of the surgeon's knife and the gnawing teeth of his saw,   930
The wheeze, the cluck, the swash of falling blood . . . . the short wild
    scream, the long dull tapering groan,
These so . . . . these irretrievable.

[37]

O Christ! My fit is mastering me!
What the rebel said gaily adjusting his throat to the rope-noose,
What the savage at the stump, his eye-sockets empty, his mouth
    spirting whoops and defiance,   935
What stills the traveler come to the vault at Mount Vernon,
What sobers the Brooklyn boy as he looks down the shores of the
    Wallabout and remembers the prison ships,
What burnt the gums of the redcoat at Saratoga when he surrendered
    his brigades,
These become mine and me every one, and they are but little,
I become as much more as I like.   940

I become any presence or truth of humanity here,
And see myself in prison shaped like another man,
And feel the dull unintermitted pain.

For me the keepers of convicts shoulder their carbines and keep
     watch,
It is I let out in the morning and barred at night.   945

Not a mutineer walks handcuffed to the jail, but I am handcuffed
     to him and walk by his side,
I am less the jolly one there, and more the silent one with sweat on
     my twitching lips.

Not a youngster is taken for larceny, but I go too and am tried and
     sentenced.

Not a cholera patient lies at the last gasp, but I also lie at the last gasp,
My face is ash-colored, my sinews gnarl . . . . away from me people
     retreat.   950

Askers embody themselves in me, and I am embodied in them,
I project my hat and sit shamefaced and beg.

I rise extatic through all, and sweep with the true gravitation,
The whirling and whirling is elemental within me.

[38]
Somehow I have been stunned. Stand back!   955
Give me a little time beyond my cuffed head and slumbers and
     dreams and gaping,
I discover myself on a verge of the usual mistake.

That I could forget the mockers and insults!
That I could forget the trickling tears and the blows of the
     bludgeons and hammers!
That I could look with a separate look on my own crucifixion and
     bloody crowning!   960

I remember . . . . I resume the overstaid fraction,
The grave of rock multiplies what has been confided to it . . . . or to
     any graves,

The corpses rise .... the gashes heal .... the fastenings roll
    away.

I troop forth replenished with supreme power, one of an average
    unending procession,
We walk the roads of Ohio and Massachusetts and Virginia and
    Wisconsin and New York and New Orleans and Texas and   965
    Montreal and San Francisco and Charleston and Savannah
    and Mexico,
Inland and by the seacoast and boundary lines .... and we pass the
    boundary lines.

Our swift ordinances are on their way over the whole earth,
The blossoms we wear in our hats are the growth of two thousand
    years.

Eleves I salute you,
I see the approach of your numberless gangs .... I see you under-
    stand yourselves and me,   970
And know that they who have eyes are divine, and the blind and
    lame are equally divine,
And that my steps drag behind yours yet go before them,
And are aware how I am with you no more than I am with
    everybody.

[39]
The friendly and flowing savage .... Who is he?
Is he waiting for civilization or past it and mastering it?   975

Is he some southwesterner raised outdoors? Is he Canadian?
Is he from the Mississippi country? or from Iowa, Oregon or
    California? or from the mountain? or prairie life or bush-life?
    or from the sea?

Wherever he goes men and women accept and desire him,
They desire he should like them and touch them and speak to them
    and stay with them.

Behaviour lawless as snow-flakes . . . . words simple as grass . . . .
　　　uncombed head and laughter and naivete;　　　　　　　980
Slowstepping feet and the common features, and the common modes
　　　and emanations,
They descend in new forms from the tips of his fingers,
They are wafted with the odor of his body or breath . . . . they fly
　　　out of the glance of his eyes.

[40]

Flaunt of the sunshine I need not your bask . . . . lie over,
You light surfaces only . . . . I force the surfaces and the depths
　　　also.　　　　　　　　　　　　　　　　　　　　　　985

Earth! you seem to look for something at my hands,
Say old topknot! what do you want?

Man or woman! I might tell how I like you, but cannot,
And might tell what it is in me and what it is in you, but cannot,
And might tell the pinings I have . . . . the pulse of my nights and
　　　days.　　　　　　　　　　　　　　　　　　　　　　990

Behold I do not give lectures or a little charity,
What I give I give out of myself.

You there, impotent, loose in the knees, open your scarfed chops till
　　　I blow grit within you,
Spread your palms and lift the flaps of your pockets,
I am not to be denied . . . . I compel . . . . I have stores plenty and
　　　to spare,　　　　　　　　　　　　　　　　　　　　995
And any thing I have I bestow.

I do not ask who you are . . . . that is not important to me,
You can do nothing and be nothing but what I will infold you.

To a drudge of the cottonfields or emptier of privies I lean . . . . on
　　　his right cheek I put the family kiss,
And in my soul I swear I never will deny him.　　　　　　1000

On women fit for conception I start bigger and nimbler babes,
This day I am jetting the stuff of far more arrogant republics.

To any one dying . . . . thither I speed and twist the knob of the door,
Turn the bedclothes toward the foot of the bed,
Let the physician and the priest go home.   1005

I seize the descending man . . . . I raise him with resistless will.

O despairer, here is my neck,
By God! you shall not go down! Hang your whole weight upon me.

I dilate you with tremendous breath . . . . I buoy you up;
Every room of the house do I fill with an armed force . . . . lovers of
    me, bafflers of graves: 1010
Sleep! I and they keep guard all night;
Not doubt, not decease shall dare to lay finger upon you,
I have embraced you, and henceforth possess you to myself,
And when you rise in the morning you will find what I tell you is so.

[41]
I am he bringing help for the sick as they pant on their backs,   1015
And for strong upright men I bring yet more needed help.

I heard what was said of the universe,
Heard it and heard of several thousand years;
It is middling well as far as it goes . . . . but is that all?

Magnifying and applying come I,   1020
Outbidding at the start the old cautious hucksters,
The most they offer for mankind and eternity less than a spirt of my
    own seminal wet,
Taking myself the exact dimensions of Jehovah and laying them away,
Lithographing Kronos and Zeus his son, and Hercules his grandson,
Buying drafts of Osiris and Isis and Belus and Brahma and Adonai, 1025
In my portfolio placing Manito loose, and Allah on a leaf, and the
    crucifix engraved,

With Odin, and the hideous-faced Mexitli, and all idols and images,
Honestly taking them all for what they are worth, and not a cent more,
Admitting they were alive and did the work of their day,
Admitting they bore mites as for unfledged birds who have now
    to rise and fly and sing for themselves,   1030
Accepting the rough deific sketches to fill out better in myself . . . .
    bestowing them freely on each man and woman I see,
Discovering as much or more in a framer framing a house,
Putting higher claims for him there with his rolled-up sleeves, driving
    the mallet and chisel;
Not objecting to special revelations . . . . considering a curl of smoke
    or a hair on the back of my hand as curious as any revelation;
Those ahold of fire-engines and hook-and-ladder ropes more to me
    than the gods of the antique wars,   1035
Minding their voices peal through the crash of destruction,
Their brawny limbs passing safe over charred laths . . . . their white
    foreheads whole and unhurt out of the flames;
By the mechanic's wife with her babe at her nipple interceding for
    every person born;
Three scythes at harvest whizzing in a row from three lusty angels
    with shirts bagged out at their waists;
The snag-toothed hostler with red hair redeeming sins past and to
    come,   1040
Selling all he possesses and traveling on foot to fee lawyers for his
    brother and sit by him while he is tried for forgery:
What was strewn in the amplest strewing the square rod about me,
    and not filling the square rod then;
The bull and the bug never worshipped half enough,
Dung and dirt more admirable than was dreamed,
The supernatural of no account . . . . myself waiting my time to be
    one of the supremes,   1045
The day getting ready for me when I shall do as much good as the
    best, and be as prodigious,
Guessing when I am it will not tickle me much to receive puffs out of
    pulpit or print;
By my life-lumps! becoming already a creator!
Putting myself here and now to the ambushed womb of the shadows!

[42]

. . . . A call in the midst of the crowd,   1050
My own voice, orotund sweeping and final.

Come my children,
Come my boys and girls, and my women and household and intimates,
Now the performer launches his nerve . . . . he has passed his
     prelude on the reeds within.

Easily written loosefingered chords! I feel the thrum of their climax
     and close.   1055

My head evolves on my neck,
Music rolls, but not from the organ . . . . folks are around me, but
     they are no household of mine.

Ever the hard and unsunk ground,
Ever the eaters and drinkers . . . . ever the upward and downward
     sun . . . . ever the air and the ceaseless tides,
Ever myself and my neighbors, refreshing and wicked and real,   1060
Ever the old inexplicable query . . . . ever that thorned thumb—that
     breath of itches and thirsts,
Ever the vexer's hoot! hoot! till we find where the sly one hides and
     bring him forth;
Ever love . . . . ever the sobbing liquid of life,
Ever the bandage under the chin . . . . ever the trestles of death.

Here and there with dimes on the eyes walking,   1065
To feed the greed of the belly the brains liberally spooning,
Tickets buying or taking or selling, but in to the feast never once
     going;
Many sweating and ploughing and thrashing, and then the chaff
     for payment receiving,
A few idly owning, and they the wheat continually claiming.

This is the city . . . . and I am one of the citizens;   1070

Whatever interests the rest interests me . . . . politics, churches,
 newspapers, schools,
Benevolent societies, improvements, banks, tariffs, steamships,
 factories, markets,
Stocks and stores and real estate and personal estate.

They who piddle and patter here in collars and tailed coats I
 am aware who they are . . . . and that they are not worms
 or fleas,
I acknowledge the duplicates of myself under all the scrape-lipped
 and pipe-legged concealments.   1075

The weakest and shallowest is deathless with me,
What I do and say the same waits for them,
Every thought that flounders in me the same flounders in them.

I know perfectly well my own egotism,
And know my omnivorous words, and cannot say any less,   1080
And would fetch you whoever you are flush with myself.

My words are words of a questioning, and to indicate reality;
This printed and bound book . . . . but the printer and the printing-
 office boy?
The marriage estate and settlement . . . . but the body and mind of
 the bridegroom? also those of the bride?
The panorama of the sea . . . . but the sea itself?   1085
The well-taken photographs . . . . but your wife or friend close and
 solid in your arms?
The fleet of ships of the line and all the modern improvements . . . .
 but the craft and pluck of the admiral?
The dishes and fare and furniture . . . . but the host and hostess, and
 the look out of their eyes?
The sky up there . . . . yet here or next door or across the way?
The saints and sages in history . . . . but you yourself?   1090
Sermons and creeds and theology . . . . but the human brain, and
 what is called reason, and what is called love, and what is
 called life?

[43]

I do not despise you priests;
My faith is the greatest of faiths and the least of faiths,
Enclosing all worship ancient and modern, and all between ancient
    and modern,
Believing I shall come again upon the earth after five thousand years, 1095
Waiting responses from oracles . . . . honoring the gods . . . .
    saluting the sun,
Making a fetish of the first rock or stump . . . . powowing with sticks
    in the circle of obis,
Helping the lama or brahmin as he trims the lamps of the idols,
Dancing yet through the streets in a phallic procession . . . . rapt and
    austere in the woods, a gymnosophist,
Drinking mead from the skull-cup . . . . to shasta and vedas
    admirant . . . . minding the koran, 1100
Walking the teokallis, spotted with gore from the stone and knife—
    beating the serpent-skin drum;
Accepting the gospels, accepting him that was crucified, knowing
    assuredly that he is divine,
To the mass kneeling—to the puritan's prayer rising—sitting
    patiently in a pew,
Ranting and frothing in my insane crisis—waiting dead-like till my
    spirit arouses me;
Looking forth on pavement and land, and outside of pavement and
    land, 1105
Belonging to the winders of the circuit of circuits.

One of that centripetal and centrifugal gang,
I turn and talk like a man leaving charges before a journey.

Down-hearted doubters, dull and excluded,
Frivolous sullen moping angry affected disheartened atheistical,
I know every one of you, and know the unspoken interrogatories, 1110
By experience I know them.

How the flukes splash!

How they contort rapid as lightning, with spasms and spouts of blood!

Be at peace bloody flukes of doubters and sullen mopers, 1115
I take my place among you as much as among any;
The past is the push of you and me and all precisely the same,
And the day and night are for you and me and all,
And what is yet untried and afterward is for you and me and all.

I do not know what is untried and afterward, 1120
But I know it is sure and alive and sufficient.

Each who passes is considered, and each who stops is considered, and
not a single one can it fail.

It cannot fail the young man who died and was buried,
Nor the young woman who died and was put by his side,
Nor the little child that peeped in at the door and then drew back
and was never seen again, 1125
Nor the old man who has lived without purpose, and feels it with
bitterness worse than gall,
Nor him in the poorhouse tubercled by rum and the bad disorder,
Nor the numberless slaughtered and wrecked . . . . nor the brutish
koboo, called the ordure of humanity,
Nor the sacs merely floating with open mouths for food to slip in,
Nor any thing in the earth, or down in the oldest graves of the earth, 1130
Nor any thing in the myriads of spheres, nor one of the myriads of
myriads that inhabit them,
Nor the present, nor the least wisp that is known.

[44]
It is time to explain myself . . . . let us stand up.

What is known I strip away . . . . I launch all men and women
forward with me into the unknown.

The clock indicates the moment . . . . but what does eternity
indicate? 1135

Eternity lies in bottomless reservoirs . . . . its buckets are rising
    forever and ever,
They pour and they pour and they exhale away.

We have thus far exhausted trillions of winters and summers;
There are trillions ahead, and trillions ahead of them.

Births have brought us richness and variety,
And other births will bring us richness and variety.   1140

I do not call one greater and one smaller,
That which fills its period and place is equal to any.

Were mankind murderous or jealous upon you my brother or my
    sister?
I am sorry for you . . . . they are not murderous or jealous
    upon me;   1145
All has been gentle with me . . . . I keep no account with
    lamentation;
What have I to do with lamentation?

I am an acme of things accomplished, and I an encloser of things
    to be.

My feet strike an apex of the apices of the stairs,
On every step bunches of ages, and larger bunches between the
    steps,   1150
All below duly traveled—and still I mount and mount.

Rise after rise bow the phantoms behind me,
Afar down I see the huge first Nothing, the vapor from the nostrils
    of death,
I know I was even there . . . . I waited unseen and always,
And slept while God carried me through the lethargic mist,   1155
And took my time . . . . and took no hurt from the fœtid carbon.

Long I was hugged close . . . . long and long.

Immense have been the preparations for me,
Faithful and friendly the arms that have helped me.

Cycles ferried my cradle, rowing and rowing like cheerful boatmen; 1160
For room to me stars kept aside in their own rings,
They sent influences to look after what was to hold me.

Before I was born out of my mother generations guided me,
My embryo has never been torpid . . . . nothing could overlay it;
For it the nebula cohered to an orb . . . . the long slow strata piled
    to rest it on . . . . vast vegetables gave it sustenance, 1165
Monstrous sauroids transported it in their mouths and deposited it
    with care.

All forces have been steadily employed to complete and delight me,
Now I stand on this spot with my soul.

[45]

Span of youth! Ever-pushed elasticity! Manhood balanced and
    florid and full!

My lovers suffocate me! 1170
Crowding my lips, and thick in the pores of my skin,
Jostling me through streets and public halls . . . . coming naked to
    me at night,
Crying by day Ahoy from the rocks of the river . . . . swinging and
    chirping over my head,
Calling my name from flowerbeds or vines or tangled underbrush,
Or while I swim in the bath . . . . or drink from the pump at the
    corner . . . . or the curtain is down at the opera . . . . or I
    glimpse at a woman's face in the railroad car; 1175
Lighting on every moment of my life,
Bussing my body with soft and balsamic busses,
Noiselessly passing handfuls out of their hearts and giving them to
    be mine.

Old age superbly rising! Ineffable grace of dying days!

Every condition promulges not only itself . . . . it promulges what
    grows after and out of itself,   1180
And the dark hush promulges as much as any.

I open my scuttle at night and see the far-sprinkled systems,
And all I see, multiplied as high as I can cipher, edge but the rim
    of the farther systems.

Wider and wider they spread, expanding and always expanding,
Outward and outward and forever outward.   1185

My sun has his sun, and round him obediently wheels,
He joins with his partners a group of superior circuit,
And greater sets follow, making specks of the greatest inside them.

There is no stoppage, and never can be stoppage;
If I and you and the worlds and all beneath or upon their surfaces,
    and all the palpable life, were this moment reduced back to a
    pallid float, it would not avail in the long run,   1190
We should surely bring up again where we now stand,
And as surely go as much farther, and then farther and farther.

A few quadrillions of eras, a few octillions of cubic leagues, do not
    hazard the span, or make it impatient,
They are but parts . . . . any thing is but a part.

See ever so far . . . . there is limitless space outside of that,   1195
Count ever so much . . . . there is limitless time around that.

Our rendezvous is fitly appointed . . . . God will be there and wait
    till we come.

[46]

I know I have the best of time and space—and that I was never
    measured, and never will be measured.

I tramp a perpetual journey,

My signs are a rain-proof coat and good shoes and a staff cut from
    the woods;   1200
No friend of mine takes his ease in my chair,
I have no chair, nor church nor philosophy;
I lead no man to a dinner-table or library or exchange,
But each man and each woman of you I lead upon a knoll,
My left hand hooks you round the waist,   1205
My right hand points to landscapes of continents, and a plain
    public road.

Not I, not any one else can travel that road for you,
You must travel it for yourself.

It is not far . . . . it is within reach,
Perhaps you have been on it since you were born, and did not
    know,   1210
Perhaps it is every where on water and on land.

Shoulder your duds, and I will mine, and let us hasten forth;
Wonderful cities and free nations we shall fetch as we go.

If you tire, give me both burdens, and rest the chuff of your hand
    on my hip,
And in due time you shall repay the same service to me;   1215
For after we start we never lie by again.

This day before dawn I ascended a hill and looked at the
    crowded heaven,
And I said to my spirit, When we become the enfolders of those
    orbs and the pleasure and knowledge of every thing in them,
    shall we be filled and satisfied then?
And my spirit said No, we level that lift to pass and continue beyond.

You are also asking me questions, and I hear you;   1220
I answer that I cannot answer . . . . you must find out for yourself.

Sit awhile wayfarer,

Here are biscuits to eat and here is milk to drink,
But as soon as you sleep and renew yourself in sweet clothes I will
    certainly kiss you with my goodbye kiss and open the gate for
    your egress hence.

Long enough have you dreamed contemptible dreams,   1225
Now I wash the gum from your eyes,
You must habit yourself to the dazzle of the light and of every
    moment of your life.

Long have you timidly waded, holding a plank by the shore,
Now I will you to be a bold swimmer,
To jump off in the midst of the sea, and rise again and nod to me
    and shout, and laughingly dash with your hair.   1230

[47]
I am the teacher of athletes,
He that by me spreads a wider breast than my own proves the
    width of my own,
He most honors my style who learns under it to destroy the teacher.

The boy I love, the same becomes a man not through derived
    power but in his own right,
Wicked, rather than virtuous out of conformity or fear,   1235
Fond of his sweetheart, relishing well his steak,
Unrequited love or a slight cutting him worse than a wound cuts,
First rate to ride, to fight, to hit the bull's eye, to sail a skiff, to
    sing a song or play on the banjo,
Preferring scars and faces pitted with smallpox over all latherers and
    those that keep out of the sun.

I teach straying from me, yet who can stray from me?   1240
I follow you whoever you are from the present hour;
My words itch at your ears till you understand them.

I do not say these things for a dollar, or to fill up the time while I
    wait for a boat;

It is you talking just as much as myself . . . . I act as the tongue of
　　you,
It was tied in your mouth . . . . in mine it begins to be loosened.　　1245

I swear I will never mention love or death inside a house,
And I swear I never will translate myself at all, only to him or her
　　who privately stays with me in the open air.

If you would understand me go to the heights or water-shore,
The nearest gnat is an explanation and a drop or the motion of
　　waves a key,
The maul the oar and the handsaw second my words.　　1250

No shuttered room or school can commune with me,
But roughs and little children better than they.

The young mechanic is closest to me . . . . he knows me pretty well,
The woodman that takes his axe and jug with him shall take me
　　with him all day,
The farmboy ploughing in the field feels good at the sound of my
　　voice,　　1255
In vessels that sail my words must sail . . . . I go with fishermen and
　　seamen, and love them,
My face rubs to the hunter's face when he lies down alone in his
　　blanket,
The driver thinking of me does not mind the jolt of his wagon,
The young mother and old mother shall comprehend me,
The girl and the wife rest the needle a moment and forget where
　　they are,　　1260
They and all would resume what I have told them.

[48]

I have said that the soul is not more than the body,
And I have said that the body is not more than the soul,
And nothing, not God, is greater to one than one's-self is,
And whoever walks a furlong without sympathy walks to his own
　　funeral, dressed in his shroud,　　1265

And I or you pocketless of a dime may purchase the pick of the earth,
And to glance with an eye or show a bean in its pod confounds the
    learning of all times,
And there is no trade or employment but the young man following
    it may become a hero,
And there is no object so soft but it makes a hub for the wheeled
    universe,
And any man or woman shall stand cool and supercilious before a
    million universes.   1270

And I call to mankind, Be not curious about God,
For I who am curious about each am not curious about God,
No array of terms can say how much I am at peace about God
    and about death.

I hear and behold God in every object, yet I understand God not
    in the least,
Nor do I understand who there can be more wonderful than myself. 1275

Why should I wish to see God better than this day?
I see something of God each hour of the twenty-four, and each
    moment then,
In the faces of men and women I see God, and in my own face in
    the glass;
I find letters from God dropped in the street, and every one is
    signed by God's name,
And I leave them where they are, for I know that others will
    punctually come forever and ever.   1280

[49]

And as to you death, and you bitter hug of mortality . . . . it is idle
    to try to alarm me.

To his work without flinching the accoucheur comes,
I see the elderhand pressing receiving supporting,
I recline by the sills of the exquisite flexible doors . . . . and mark
    the outlet, and mark the relief and escape.

And as to you corpse I think you are good manure, but that does
    not offend me,   1285
I smell the white roses sweetscented and growing,
I reach to the leafy lips . . . . I reach to the polished breasts of
    melons,

And as to you life, I reckon you are the leavings of many deaths,
No doubt I have died myself ten thousand times before.

I hear you whispering there O stars of heaven,   1290
O suns . . . . O grass of graves . . . . O perpetual transfers and
    promotions . . . . if you do not say anything how can I say
    anything?

Of the turbid pool that lies in the autumn forest,
Of the moon that descends the steeps of the soughing twilight,
Toss, sparkles of day and dusk . . . . toss on the black stems that
    decay in the muck,
Toss to the moaning gibberish of the dry limbs.   1295

I ascend from the moon . . . . I ascend from the night,
And perceive of the ghastly glitter the sunbeams reflected,
And debouch to the steady and central from the offspring great or
    small.

[50]
There is that in me . . . . I do not know what it is . . . . but I know
    it is in me.

Wrenched and sweaty . . . . calm and cool then my body becomes; 1300
I sleep . . . . I sleep long.

I do not know it . . . . it is without name . . . . it is a word unsaid,
It is not in any dictionary or utterance or symbol.

Something it swings on more than the earth I swing on,
To it the creation is the friend whose embracing awakes me.   1305

Perhaps I might tell more . . . . Outlines! I plead for my brothers
 and sisters.

Do you see O my brothers and sisters?
It is not chaos or death . . . . it is form and union and plan . . . . it
 is eternal life . . . . it is happiness.

[51]

The past and present wilt . . . . I have filled them and emptied
 them,
And proceed to fill my next fold of the future.   1310

Listener up there! Here you . . . . what have you to confide to me?
Look in my face while I snuff the sidle of evening,
Talk honestly, for no one else hears you, and I stay only a minute
 longer.

Do I contradict myself?
Very well then . . . . I contradict myself;   1315
I am large . . . . I contain multitudes.

I concentrate toward them that are nigh . . . . I wait on the door-slab.

Who has done his day's work and will soonest be through with his
 supper?
Who wishes to walk with me?

Will you speak before I am gone? Will you prove already too late? 1320

[52]

The spotted hawk swoops by and accuses me . . . . he complains of
 my gab and my loitering.

I too am not a bit tamed . . . . I too am untranslatable,
I sound my barbaric yawp over the roofs of the world.

The last scud of day holds back for me,

It flings my likeness after the rest and true as any on the shadowed
    wilds,   1325
It coaxes me to the vapor and the dusk.

I depart as air . . . . I shake my white locks at the runaway sun,
I effuse my flesh in eddies and drift it in lacy jags.

I bequeath myself to the dirt to grow from the grass I love,
If you want me again look for me under your bootsoles.   1330

You will hardly know who I am or what I mean,
But I shall be good health to you nevertheless,
And filter and fibre your blood.

Failing to fetch me me at first keep encouraged,
Missing me one place search another,   1335
I stop some where waiting for you

LEAVES OF GRASS

[*A Song for Occupations*]

[1]

COME CLOSER TO ME,
Push close my lovers and take the best I possess,
Yield closer and closer and give me the best you possess.

This is unfinished business with me . . . . how is it with you?
I was chilled with the cold types and cylinder and wet paper
    between us.

I pass so poorly with paper and types . . . . I must pass with the
    contact of bodies and souls.

I do not thank you for liking me as I am, and liking the touch of
    me . . . . I know that it is good for you to do so.

Were all educations practical and ornamental well displayed out of
    me, what would it amount to?
Were I as the head teacher or charitable proprietor or wise states-
    man, what would it amount to?
Were I to you as the boss employing and paying you, would that
    satisfy you?

The learned and virtuous and benevolent, and the usual terms;
A man like me, and never the usual terms.

Neither a servant nor a master am I,
I take no sooner a large price than a small price . . . . I will have
    my own whoever enjoys me,

I will be even with you, and you shall be even with me.   15

If you are a workman or workwoman I stand as nigh as the nighest
    that works in the same shop,
If you bestow gifts on your brother or dearest friend, I demand as
    good as your brother or dearest friend,
If your lover or husband or wife is welcome by day or night, I must
    be personally as welcome;
If you have become degraded or ill, then I will become so for your
    sake;
If you remember your foolish and outlawed deeds, do you think I
    cannot remember my foolish and outlawed deeds?   20
If you carouse at the table I say I will carouse at the opposite side of
    the table;
If you meet some stranger in the street and love him or her, do I
    not often meet strangers in the street and love them?
If you see a good deal remarkable in me I see just as much remark-
    able in you.

Why what have you thought of yourself?
Is it you then that thought yourself less?   25
Is it you that thought the President greater than you? or the rich
    better off than you? or the educated wiser than you?

Because you are greasy or pimpled—or that you was once drunk, or
    a thief, or diseased, or rheumatic, or a prostitute—or are so
    now—or from frivolity or impotence—or that you are no
    scholar, and never saw your name in print . . . . do you give in
    that you are any less immortal?

[2]

Souls of men and women! it is not you I call unseen, unheard,
    untouchable and untouching;
It is not you I go argue pro and con about, and to settle whether
    you are alive or no;
I own publicly who you are, if nobody else owns . . . . and see and
    hear you, and what you give and take;   30

What is there you cannot give and take?

I see not merely that you are polite or whitefaced . . . . married or
    single . . . . citizens of old states or citizens of new states . . . .
    eminent in some profession . . . . a lady or gentleman in a
    parlor . . . . or dressed in the jail uniform . . . . or pulpit
    uniform,
Not only the free Utahan, Kansian, or Arkansian . . . . not only the
    free Cuban . . . not merely the slave . . . . not Mexican
    native, or Flatfoot, or negro from Africa,
Iroquois eating the warflesh—fishtearer in his lair of rocks and
    sand . . . . Esquimaux in the dark cold snowhouse . . . . Chinese
    with his transverse eyes . . . . Bedowee—or wandering nomad—
    or tabounschik at the head of his droves,
Grown, half-grown, and babe—of this country and every country,
    indoors and outdoors I see . . . . and all else is behind or
    through them.   35

The wife—and she is not one jot less than the husband,
The daughter—and she is just as good as the son,
The mother—and she is every bit as much as the father.

Offspring of those not rich—boys apprenticed to trades,
Young fellows working on farms and old fellows working on farms;   40
The naive . . . . the simple and hardy . . . . he going to the polls to
    vote . . . . he who has a good time, and he who has a bad
    time;
Mechanics, southerners, new arrivals, sailors, mano'warsmen,
    merchantmen, coasters,
All these I see . . . . but nigher and farther the same I see;
None shall escape me, and none shall wish to escape me.

I bring what you much need, yet always have,   45
I bring not money or amours or dress or eating . . . . but I bring as
    good;
And send no agent or medium . . . . and offer no representative of
    value—but offer the value itself.

There is something that comes home to one now and perpetually,
It is not what is printed or preached or discussed . . . . it eludes
    discussion and print,
It is not to be put in a book . . . . it is not in this book,   50
It is for you whoever you are . . . . it is no farther from you than
    your hearing and sight are from you,
It is hinted by nearest and commonest and readiest . . . . it is not
    them, though it is endlessly provoked by them . . . . What is
    there ready and near you now?

You may read in many languages and read nothing about it;
You may read the President's message and read nothing about it
    there;
Nothing in the reports from the state department or treasury
    department . . . . or in the daily papers, or the weekly papers,   55
Or in the census returns or assessors' returns or prices current or any
    accounts of stock.

[3]

The sun and stars that float in the open air . . . . the appleshaped
    earth and we upon it . . . . surely the drift of them is something
    grand;
I do not know what it is except that it is grand, and that it is
    happiness,
And that the enclosing purport of us here is not a speculation, or
    bon-mot or reconnoissance,
And that it is not something which by luck may turn out well for us,
    and without luck must be a failure for us,   60
And not something which may yet be retracted in a certain
    contingency.

The light and shade—the curious sense of body and identity—the
    greed that with perfect complaisance devours all things—the
    endless pride and outstretching of man—unspeakable joys and
    sorrows,
The wonder every one sees in every one else he sees . . . . and the
    wonders that fill each minute of time forever and each acre of
    surface and space forever,

Have you reckoned them as mainly for a trade or farmwork? or for
 the profits of a store? or to achieve yourself a position? or to fill
 a gentleman's leisure or a lady's leisure?

Have you reckoned the landscape took substance and form that it
 might be painted in a picture? 65
Or men and women that they might be written of, and songs sung?
Or the attraction of gravity and the great laws and harmonious
 combinations and the fluids of the air as subjects for the savans?
Or the brown land and the blue sea for maps and charts?
Or the stars to be put in constellations and named fancy names?
Or that the growth of seeds is for agricultural tables or agriculture
 itself? 70

Old institutions . . . . these arts libraries legends collections—and the
 practice handed along in manufactures . . . . will we rate them
 so high?
Will we rate our prudence and business so high? . . . . I have no
 objection,
I rate them as high as the highest . . . . but a child born of a woman
 and man I rate beyond all rate.

We thought our Union grand and our Constitution grand;
I do not say they are not grand and good—for they are, 75
I am this day just as much in love with them as you,
But I am eternally in love with you and with all my fellows upon
 the earth.

We consider the bibles and religions divine . . . . I do not say they
 are not divine,
I say they have all grown out of you and may grow out of you still,
It is not they who give the life . . . . it is you who give the life; 80
Leaves are not more shed from the trees or trees from the earth than
 they are shed out of you.

[4]
The sum of all known value and respect I add up in you whoever
 you are;

The President is up there in the White House for you . . . . it is not
    you who are here for him,
The Secretaries act in their bureaus for you . . . . not you here for
    them,
The Congress convenes every December for you,   85
Laws, courts, the forming of states, the charters of cities, the going
    and coming of commerce and mails are all for you.

All doctrines, all politics and civilization exurge from you,
All sculpture and monuments and anything inscribed anywhere are
    tallied in you,
The gist of histories and statistics as far back as the records reach is
    in you this hour—and myths and tales the same;
If you were not breathing and walking here where would they all be? 90
The most renowned poems would be ashes . . . . orations and plays
    would be vacuums.

All architecture is what you do to it when you look upon it;
Did you think it was in the white or gray stone? or the lines of the
    arches and cornices?

All music is what awakens from you when you are reminded by the
    instruments,
It is not the violins and the cornets . . . . it is not the oboe nor the
    beating drums—nor the notes of the baritone singer singing his
    sweet romanza . . . . nor those of the men's chorus, nor those of
    the women's chorus,   95
It is nearer and farther than they.

[5]
Will the whole come back then?
Can each see the signs of the best by a look in the lookingglass? Is
    there nothing greater or more?
Does all sit there with you and here with me?

The old forever new things . . . . you foolish child! . . . . the closest
    simplest things—this moment with you,   100

Your person and every particle that relates to your person,
The pulses of your brain waiting their chance and encouragement
    at every deed or sight;
Anything you do in public by day, and anything you do in secret
    betweendays,
What is called right and what is called wrong . . . . what you
    behold or touch . . . . what causes your anger or wonder,
The anklechain of the slave, the bed of the bedhouse, the cards of
    the gambler, the plates of the forger;   105
What is seen or learned in the street, or intuitively learned,
What is learned in the public school—spelling, reading, writing and
    ciphering . . . . the blackboard and the teacher's diagrams:
The panes of the windows and all that appears through them . . . .
    the going forth in the morning and the aimless spending of the
    day;
(What is it that you made money? what is it that you got what you
    wanted?)
The usual routine . . . . the workshop, factory, yard, office, store, or
    desk;   110
The jaunt of hunting or fishing, or the life of hunting or fishing,
Pasturelife, foddering, milking and herding, and all the personnel
    and usages;
The plum-orchard and apple-orchard . . . . gardening . . . . seedlings,
    cuttings, flowers and vines,
Grains and manures . . marl, clay, loam . . the subsoil plough . . the
    shovel and pick and rake and hoe . . irrigation and draining;
The currycomb . . the horse-cloth . . the halter and bridle and bits
    . . the very wisps of straw,   115
The barn and barn-yard . . the bins and mangers . . the mows and
    racks:
Manufactures . . commerce . . engineering . . the building of cities,
    and every trade carried on there . . and the implements of
    every trade,
The anvil and tongs and hammer . . the axe and wedge . . the
    square and mitre and jointer and smoothingplane;
The plumbob and trowel and level . . the wall-scaffold, and the
    work of walls and ceilings . . or any mason-work:

The ship's compass . . the sailor's tarpaulin . . the stays and lan-
yards, and the ground-tackle for anchoring or mooring,   120
The sloop's tiller . . the pilot's wheel and bell . . the yacht or fish-
smack . . the great gay-pennanted three-hundred-foot steamboat under full headway, with her proud fat breasts and her
delicate swift-flashing paddles;
The trail and line and hooks and sinkers . . the seine, and hauling
the seine;
Smallarms and rifles . . . . the powder and shot and caps and
wadding . . . . the ordnance for war . . . . the carriages:
Everyday objects . . . . the housechairs, the carpet, the bed and the
counterpane of the bed, and him or her sleeping at night, and
the wind blowing, and the indefinite noises:
The snowstorm or rainstorm . . . . the tow-trowsers . . . . the lodge-
hut in the woods, and the still-hunt: 125
City and country . . fireplace and candle . . gaslight and
heater and aqueduct;
The message of the governor, mayor, or chief of police . . . . the
dishes of breakfast or dinner or supper;
The bunkroom, the fire-engine, the string-team, and the car or
truck behind;
The paper I write on or you write on . . and every word we write . .
and every cross and twirl of the pen . . and the curious way we
write what we think . . . . yet very faintly;
The directory, the detector, the ledger . . . . the books in ranks or
the bookshelves . . . . the clock attached to the wall,   130
The ring on your finger . . the lady's wristlet . . the hammers of
stonebreakers or coppersmiths . . the druggist's vials and
jars;
The etui of surgical instruments, and the etui of oculist's or aurist's
instruments, or dentist's instruments;
Glassblowing, grinding of wheat and corn . . casting, and what is
cast . . tinroofing, shingledressing,
Shipcarpentering, flagging of sidewalks by flaggers . . dockbuilding,
fishcuring, ferrying;
The pump, the piledriver, the great derrick . . the coalkiln and
brickkiln,   135

Ironworks or whiteleadworks .. the sugarhouse .. steam-saws,
    and the great mills and factories;
The cottonbale .. the stevedore's hook .. the saw and buck of the
    sawyer .. the screen of the coalscreener .. the mould of the
    moulder .. the workingknife of the butcher;
The cylinder press .. the handpress .. the frisket and tympan .. the
    compositor's stick and rule,
The implements for daguerreotyping . . . . the tools of the rigger or
    grappler or sailmaker or blockmaker,
Goods of guttapercha or papiermache . . . . colors and brushes . . . .
    glaziers' implements,   140
The veneer and gluepot .. the confectioner's ornaments .. the
    decanter and glasses .. the shears and flatiron;
The awl and kneestrap .. the pint measure and quart measure .. the
    counter and stool .. the writingpen of quill or metal;
Billiards and tenpins . . . . the ladders and hanging ropes of the
    gymnasium, and the manly exercises;
The designs for wallpapers or oilcloths or carpets . . . . the fancies for
    goods for women . . . . the bookbinder's stamps;
Leatherdressing, coachmaking, boilermaking, ropetwisting, distilling,
    signpainting, limeburning, coopering, cottonpicking,   145
The walkingbeam of the steam-engine .. the throttle and governors,
    and the up and down rods,
Stavemachines and planingmachines . . . . the cart of the carman
    .. the omnibus .. the ponderous dray;
The snowplough and two engines pushing it . . . . the ride in the
    express train of only one car . . . . the swift go through a
    howling storm:
The bearhunt or coonhunt . . . . the bonfire of shavings in the open
    lot in the city .. the crowd of children watching;
The blows of the fighting-man .. the upper cut and one-two-three;   150
The shopwindows . . . . the coffins in the sexton's wareroom . . . . the
    fruit on the fruitstand . . . . the beef on the butcher's stall,
The bread and cakes in the bakery . . . . the white and red pork in
    the pork-store;
The milliner's ribbons .. the dressmaker's patterns . . . . the tea-
    table .. the homemade sweetmeats:

The column of wants in the one-cent paper . . the news by telegraph
    . . . . the amusements and operas and shows:
The cotton and woolen and linen you wear . . . . the money you
    make and spend;   155
Your room and bedroom . . . . your piano-forte . . . . the stove and
    cookpans,
The house you live in . . . . the rent . . . . the other tenants . . . . the
    deposit in the savings-bank . . . . the trade at the grocery,
The pay on Saturday night . . . . the going home, and the purchases;
In them the heft of the heaviest . . . . in them far more than you
    estimated, and far less also,
In them, not yourself . . . . you and your soul enclose all things,
    regardless of estimation,   160
In them your themes and hints and provokers . . if not, the whole
    earth has no themes or hints or provokers, and never had.

I do not affirm what you see beyond is futile . . . . I do not advise
    you to stop,
I do not say leadings you thought great are not great,
But I say that none lead to greater or sadder or happier than those
    lead to.

[6]
Will you seek afar off? You surely come back at last,
In things best known to you finding the best or as good as
    the best,   165
In folks nearest to you finding also the sweetest and strongest and
    lovingest,
Happiness not in another place, but this place . . not for another
    hour, but this hour,
Man in the first you see or touch . . . . always in your friend or
    brother or nighest neighbor . . . . Woman in your mother or
    lover or wife,
And all else thus far known giving place to men and women.   170

When the psalm sings instead of the singer,
When the script preaches instead of the preacher,

When the pulpit descends and goes instead of the carver that
    carved the supporting desk,
When the sacred vessels or the bits of the eucharist, or the lath and
    plast, procreate as effectually as the young silversmiths or
    bakers, or the masons in their overalls,
When a university course convinces like a slumbering woman and
    child convince,   175
When the minted gold in the vault smiles like the nightwatchman's
    daughter,
When warrantee deeds loafe in chairs opposite and are my friendly
    companions,
I intend to reach them my hand and make as much of them as I do
    of men and women.

LEAVES OF GRASS

[To Think of Time]

[1]

To THINK OF TIME . . . . TO THINK THROUGH THE RETROSPECTION,
To think of today . . and the ages continued henceforward.
Have you guessed you yourself would not continue? Have you
    dreaded those earth-beetles?
Have you feared the future would be nothing to you?

Is today nothing? Is the beginningless past nothing?   5
If the future is nothing they are just as surely nothing.

To think that the sun rose in the east . . . . that men and women
    were flexible and real and alive . . . . that every thing was real
    and alive;
To think that you and I did not see feel think nor bear our part,
To think that we are now here and bear our part.

[2]

Not a day passes . . not a minute or second without an accouche-
    ment;   10
Not a day passes . . not a minute or second without a corpse.

When the dull nights are over, and the dull days also,
When the soreness of lying so much in bed is over,
When the physician, after long putting off, gives the silent and
    terrible look for an answer,
When the children come hurried and weeping, and the brothers
    and sisters have been sent for,   15

When medicines stand unused on the shelf, and the camphor-smell
    has pervaded the rooms,
When the faithful hand of the living does not desert the hand of the
    dying,
When the twitching lips press lightly on the forehead of the dying,
When the breath ceases and the pulse of the heart ceases,
Then the corpse-limbs stretch on the bed, and the living look upon
    them,   20
They are palpable as the living are palpable.

The living look upon the corpse with their eyesight,
But without eyesight lingers a different living and looks curiously on
    the corpse.

[3]

To think that the rivers will come to flow, and the snow fall, and
    fruits ripen . . and act upon others as upon us now . . . . yet
    not act upon us;
To think of all these wonders of city and country . . and others
    taking great interest in them . . and we taking small interest
    in them.   25

To think how eager we are in building our houses,
To think others shall be just as eager . . and we quite indifferent.

I see one building the house that serves him a few years . . . . or
    seventy or eighty years at most;
I see one building the house that serves him longer than that.

Slowmoving and black lines creep over the whole earth . . . . they
    never cease . . . . they are the burial lines,   30
He that was President was buried, and he that is now President
    shall surely be buried.

[4]

Cold dash of waves at the ferrywharf,
Posh and ice in the river . . . . half-frozen mud in the streets,

A gray discouraged sky overhead . . . . the short last daylight of
    December,
A hearse and stages . . . . other vehicles give place,   35
The funeral of an old stagedriver . . . . the cortege mostly drivers.

Rapid the trot to the cemetery,
Duly rattles the deathbell . . . . the gate is passed . . . . the grave is
    halted at . . . . the living alight . . . . the hearse uncloses,
The coffin is lowered and settled . . . . the whip is laid on the coffin,
The earth is swiftly shovelled in . . . . a minute . . no one moves or
    speaks . . . . it is done,   40
He is decently put away . . . . is there anything more?

He was a goodfellow,
Freemouthed, quicktempered, not badlooking, able to take his own
    part,
Witty, sensitive to a slight, ready with life or death for a friend,
Fond of women, . . played some . . eat hearty and drank hearty,   45
Had known what it was to be flush . . grew lowspirited toward the
    last . . sickened . . was helped by a contribution,
Died aged forty-one years . . and that was his funeral.

Thumb extended or finger uplifted,
Apron, cape, gloves, strap . . . . wetweather clothes . . . . whip
    carefully chosen . . . . boss, spotter, starter, and hostler,
Somebody loafing on you, or you loafing on somebody . . . . head-
    way . . . . man before and man behind,   50
Good day's work or bad day's work . . . . pet stock or mean stock
    . . . . first out or last out . . . . turning in at night,
To think that these are so much and so nigh to other drivers . . . .
    and he there takes no interest in them.

[5]

The markets, the government, the workingman's wages . . . . to
    think what account they are through our nights and days;
To think that other workingmen will make just as great account of
    them . . yet we make little or no account.

The vulgar and the refined . . . . what you call sin and what you
    call goodness . . to think how wide a difference; 55
To think the difference will still continue to others, yet we lie
    beyond the difference.

To think how much pleasure there is!
Have you pleasure from looking at the sky? Have you pleasure
    from poems?
Do you enjoy yourself in the city? or engaged in business? or
    planning a nomination and election? or with your wife and
    family?
Or with your mother and sisters? or in womanly housework? or
    the beautiful maternal cares? 60

These also flow onward to others . . . . you and I flow onward;
But in due time you and I shall take less interest in them.

Your farm and profits and crops . . . . to think how engrossed you
    are;
To think there will still be farms and profits and crops . . yet for
    you of what avail?

[6]
What will be will be well—for what is is well, 65
To take interest is well, and not to take interest shall be well.

The sky continues beautiful . . . . the pleasure of men with women
    shall never be sated . . nor the pleasure of women with men
    . . nor the pleasure from poems;
The domestic joys, the daily housework or business, the building of
    houses—they are not phantasms . . they have weight and
    form and location;
The farms and profits and crops . . the markets and wages and
    government . . they also are not phantasms; 70
The difference between sin and goodness is no apparition;
The earth is not an echo . . . . man and his life and all the things
    of his life are well-considered.

You are not thrown to the winds . . you gather certainly and
　　safely around yourself,
Yourself! Yourself! Yourself forever and ever!

[7]

It is not to diffuse you that you were born of your mother and
　　father—it is to identify you,　　　　　　　　　　　　　　　　75
It is not that you should be undecided, but that you should be
　　decided;
Something long preparing and formless is arrived and formed in you,
You are thenceforth secure, whatever comes or goes.

The threads that were spun are gathered . . . . the weft crosses the
　　warp . . . . the pattern is systematic.

The preparations have every one been justified;　　　　　　　　80
The orchestra have tuned their instruments sufficiently . . . . the
　　baton has given the signal.

The guest that was coming . . . . he waited long for reasons . . . . he
　　is now housed,
He is one of those who are beautiful and happy . . . . he is one of
　　those that to look upon and be with is enough.

The law of the past cannot be eluded,
The law of the present and future cannot be eluded,　　　　　　85
The law of the living cannot be eluded . . . . it is eternal,
The law of promotion and transformation cannot be eluded,
The law of heroes and good-doers cannot be eluded,
The law of drunkards and informers and mean persons cannot be
　　eluded.

[8]

Slowmoving and black lines go ceaselessly over the earth,　　　90
Northerner goes carried and southerner goes carried . . . and they on
　　the Atlantic side and they on the Pacific, and they between, and
　　all through the Mississippi country . . . . and all over the earth.

The great masters and kosmos are well as they go . . . . the heroes
    and good-doers are well,
The known leaders and inventors and the rich owners and pious and
    distinguished may be well,
But there is more account than that . . . . there is strict account
    of all.

The interminable hordes of the ignorant and wicked are not nothing,   95
The barbarians of Africa and Asia are not nothing,
The common people of Europe are not nothing . . . . the American
    aborigines are not nothing,
A zambo or a foreheadless Crowfoot or a Camanche is not nothing,
The infected in the immigrant hospital are not nothing . . . . the
    murderer or mean person is not nothing,
The perpetual succession of shallow people are not nothing as they
    go,   100
The prostitute is not nothing . . . . the mocker of religion is not
    nothing as he goes.

I shall go with the rest . . . . we have satisfaction:
I have dreamed that we are not to be changed so much . . . . nor
    the law of us changed;
I have dreamed that heroes and good-doers shall be under the
    present and past law,
And that murderers and drunkards and liars shall be under the
    present and past law;   105
For I have dreamed that the law they are under now is enough.

And I have dreamed that the satisfaction is not so much changed
    . . . . and that there is no life without satisfaction;
What is the earth? what are body and soul without satisfaction?

I shall go with the rest,
We cannot be stopped at a given point . . . . that is no satisfaction;   110
To show us a good thing or a few good things for a space of time —
    that is no satisfaction;
We must have the indestructible breed of the best, regardless of time.

If otherwise, all these things came but to ashes of dung;
If maggots and rats ended us, then suspicion and treachery and death.

Do you suspect death? If I were to suspect death I should die now,　　115
Do you think I could walk pleasantly and well-suited toward
　　annihilation?

Pleasantly and well-suited I walk,
Whither I walk I cannot define, but I know it is good,
The whole universe indicates that it is good,
The past and the present indicate that it is good.　　　　　　　120

How beautiful and perfect are the animals! How perfect is my soul!
How perfect the earth, and the minutest thing upon it!
What is called good is perfect, and what is called sin is just as perfect;
The vegetables and minerals are all perfect . . and the imponderable
　　fluids are perfect;
Slowly and surely they have passed on to this, and slowly and surely
　　they will yet pass on.　　　　　　　　　　　　　　　125

O my soul! if I realize you I have satisfaction,
Animals and vegetables! if I realize you I have satisfaction,
Laws of the earth and air! if I realize you I have satisfaction.

I cannot define my satisfaction . . yet it is so,
I cannot define my life . . yet it is so.　　　　　　　　　130

[9]
I swear I see now that every thing has an eternal soul!
The trees have, rooted in the ground . . . . the weeds of the sea
　　have . . . . the animals.

I swear I think there is nothing but immortality!
That the exquisite scheme is for it, and the nebulous float is for it,
　　and the cohering is for it,
And all preparation is for it . . and identity is for it . . and life and
　　death are for it.　　　　　　　　　　　　　　　　135

LEAVES OF GRASS

[*The Sleepers*]

[1]

I WANDER ALL NIGHT IN MY VISION,
Stepping with light feet . . . . swiftly and noiselessly stepping and
    stopping,
Bending with open eyes over the shut eyes of sleepers;
Wandering and confused . . . . lost to myself . . . . ill-assorted . . . .
    contradictory,
Pausing and gazing and bending and stopping. 5

How solemn they look there, stretched and still;
How quiet they breathe, the little children in their cradles.

The wretched features of ennuyees, the white features of corpses, the
    livid faces of drunkards, the sick-gray faces of onanists,
The gashed bodies on battlefields, the insane in their strong-doored
    rooms, the sacred idiots,
The newborn emerging from gates and the dying emerging from
    gates, 10
The night pervades them and enfolds them.

The married couple sleep calmly in their bed, he with his palm on
    the hip of the wife, and she with her palm on the hip of the
    husband,
The sisters sleep lovingly side by side in their bed,
The men sleep lovingly side by side in theirs,
And the mother sleeps with her little child carefully wrapped. 15

The blind sleep, and the deaf and dumb sleep,
The prisoner sleeps well in the prison . . . . the runaway son sleeps,
The murderer that is to be hung next day . . . . how does he sleep?
And the murdered person . . . . how does he sleep?

The female that loves unrequited sleeps,   20
And the male that loves unrequited sleeps;
The head of the moneymaker that plotted all day sleeps,
And the enraged and treacherous dispositions sleep.

I stand with drooping eyes by the worstsuffering and restless,
I pass my hands soothingly to and fro a few inches from them;   25
The restless sink in their beds . . . . they fitfully sleep.

The earth recedes from me into the night,
I saw that it was beautiful . . . . and I see that what is not the earth
    is beautiful.

I go from bedside to bedside . . . . I sleep close with the other
    sleepers, each in turn;
I dream in my dream all the dreams of the other dreamers,   30
And I become the other dreamers.

I am a dance . . . . Play up there! the fit is whirling me fast.

I am the everlaughing . . . . it is new moon and twilight,
I see the hiding of douceurs . . . . I see nimble ghosts whichever
    way I look,
Cache and cache again deep in the ground and sea, and where it is
    neither ground or sea.   35

Well do they do their jobs, those journeymen divine,
Only from me can they hide nothing and would not if they could;
I reckon I am their boss, and they make me a pet besides,
And surround me, and lead me and run ahead when I walk,
And lift their cunning covers and signify me with stretched arms, and
    resume the way;   40

Onward we move, a gay gang of blackguards with mirthshouting
    music and wildflapping pennants of joy.

I am the actor and the actress . . . . the voter . . the politician,
The emigrant and the exile . . the criminal that stood in the box,
He who has been famous, and he who shall be famous after today,
The stammerer . . . . the wellformed person . . the wasted or feeble
    person.   45

I am she who adorned herself and folded her hair expectantly,
My truant lover has come and it is dark.

Double yourself and receive me darkness,
Receive me and my lover too . . . . he will not let me go without him.

I roll myself upon you as upon a bed . . . . I resign myself to the dusk. 50

He whom I call answers me and takes the place of my lover,
He rises with me silently from the bed.

Darkness you are gentler than my lover . . . . his flesh was sweaty
    and panting,
I feel the hot moisture yet that he left me.

My hands are spread forth . . I pass them in all directions,   55
I would sound up the shadowy shore to which you are journeying.

Be careful, darkness . . . . already, what was it touched me?
I thought my lover had gone . . . . else darkness and he are one,
I hear the heart-beat . . . . I follow . . I fade away.

O hotcheeked and blushing! O foolish hectic!   60
O for pity's sake, no one must see me now! . . . . my clothes were
    stolen while I was abed,
Now I am thrust forth, where shall I run?

Pier that I saw dimly last night when I looked from the windows,

Pier out from the main, let me catch myself with you and stay I
    will not chafe you;
I feel ashamed to go naked about the world,   65
And am curious to know where my feet stand . . . . and what is this
    flooding me, childhood or manhood . . . . and the hunger that
    crosses the bridge between.

The cloth laps a first sweet eating and drinking,
Laps life-swelling yolks . . . . laps ear of rose-corn, milky and just
    ripened:
The white teeth stay, and the boss-tooth advances in darkness,
And liquor is spilled on lips and bosoms by touching glasses, and the
    best liquor afterward.   70

[2]

I descend my western course . . . . my sinews are flaccid,
Perfume and youth course through me, and I am their wake.

It is my face yellow and wrinkled instead of the old woman's,
I sit low in a strawbottom chair and carefully darn my grandson's
    stockings.

It is I too . . . . the sleepless widow looking out on the winter
    midnight,   75
I see the sparkles of starshine on the icy and pallid earth.

A shroud I see—and I am the shroud . . . . I wrap a body and lie in
    the coffin;
It is dark here underground . . . . it is not evil or pain here . . . . it is
    blank here, for reasons.

It seems to me that everything in the light and air ought to be
    happy;
Whoever is not in his coffin and the dark grave, let him know he
    has enough.   80

[3]

I see a beautiful gigantic swimmer swimming naked through the
    eddies of the sea,
His brown hair lies close and even to his head . . . . he strikes out
    with courageous arms . . . . he urges himself with his legs.

I see his white body . . . . I see his undaunted eyes;
I hate the swift-running eddies that would dash him headforemost
    on the rocks.

What are you doing you ruffianly red-trickled waves?   85
Will you kill the courageous giant? Will you kill him in the prime
    of his middle age?

Steady and long he struggles;
He is baffled and banged and bruised . . . . he holds out while his
    strength holds out,
The slapping eddies are spotted with his blood . . . . they bear him
    away . . . . they roll him and swing him and turn him:
His beautiful body is borne in the circling eddies . . . . it is continually
    bruised on rocks,   90
Swiftly and out of sight is borne the brave corpse.

[4]

I turn but do not extricate myself;
Confused . . . . a pastreading . . . . another, but with darkness yet.

The beach is cut by the razory ice-wind . . . . the wreck-guns sounds,
The tempest lulls and the moon comes floundering through the drifts. 95

I look where the ship helplessly heads end on . . . . I hear the burst
    as she strikes . . I hear the howls of dismay . . . . they grow
    fainter and fainter.

I cannot aid with my wringing fingers;
I can but rush to the surf and let it drench me and freeze upon me.

I search with the crowd . . . . not one of the company is washed to
    us alive;
In the morning I help pick up the dead and lay them in rows in a
    barn.   100

[5]

Now of the old war-days . . the defeat at Brooklyn;
Washington stands inside the lines . . he stands on the entrenched
    hills amid a crowd of officers,
His face is cold and damp . . . . he cannot repress the weeping
    drops . . . . he lifts the glass perpetually to his eyes . . . . the
    color is blanched from his cheeks,
He sees the slaughter of the southern braves confided to him by their
    parents.

The same at last and at last when peace is declared,   105
He stands in the room of the old tavern . . . . the wellbeloved
    soldiers all pass through.

The officers speechless and slow draw near in their turns,
The chief encircles their necks with his arm and kisses them on the
    cheek,
He kisses lightly the wet cheeks one after another . . . . he shakes
    hands and bids goodbye to the army.

[6]

Now I tell what my mother told me today as we sat at dinner
    together,   110
Of when she was a nearly grown girl living home with her parents on
    the old homestead.

A red squaw came one breakfastime to the old homestead,
On her back she carried a bundle of rushes for rushbottoming chairs;
Her hair straight shiny coarse black and profuse halfenveloped her
    face,
Her step was free and elastic . . . . her voice sounded exquisitely as
    she spoke.   115

My mother looked in delight and amazement at the stranger,
She looked at the beauty of her tallborne face and full and pliant
limbs,
The more she looked upon her she loved her,
Never before had she seen such wonderful beauty and purity;
She made her sit on a bench by the jamb of the fireplace . . . . she
cooked food for her,   120
She had no work to give her but she gave her remembrance and
fondness.

The red squaw staid all the forenoon, and toward the middle of the
afternoon she went away;
O my mother was loth to have her go away,
All the week she thought of her . . . . she watched for her many a
month,
She remembered her many a winter and many a summer,   125
But the red squaw never came nor was heard of there again.

Now Lucifer was not dead . . . . or if he was I am his sorrowful
terrible heir;
I have been wronged . . . . I am oppressed . . . . I hate him that
oppresses me,
I will either destroy him, or he shall release me.

Damn him! how he does defile me,   130
How he informs against my brother and sister and takes pay for
their blood,
How he laughs when I look down the bend after the steamboat that
carries away my woman.

Now the vast dusk bulk that is the whale's bulk . . . . it seems mine,
Warily, sportsman! though I lie so sleepy and sluggish, my tap is
death.

[7]
A show of the summer softness . . . . a contact of something unseen
. . . . an amour of the light and air;   135

I am jealous and overwhelmed with friendliness,
And will go gallivant with the light and the air myself,
And have an unseen something to be in contact with them also.

O love and summer! you are in the dreams and in me,
Autumn and winter are in the dreams . . . . the farmer goes with
    his thrift,   140
The droves and crops increase . . . . the barns are wellfilled.

Elements merge in the night . . . . ships make tacks in the dreams
    . . . . the sailor sails . . . . the exile returns home,
The fugitive returns unharmed . . . . the immigrant is back beyond
    months and years;
The poor Irishman lives in the simple house of his childhood, with
    the wellknown neighbors and faces,
They warmly welcome him . . . . he is barefoot again . . . . he
    forgets he is welloff;   145
The Dutchman voyages home, and the Scotchman and Welchman
    voyage home . . and the native of the Mediterranean voyages
    home;
To every port of England and France and Spain enter wellfilled
    ships;
The Swiss foots it toward his hills . . . . the Prussian goes his way,
    and the Hungarian his way, and the Pole goes his way,
The Swede returns, and the Dane and Norwegian return.

The homeward bound and the outward bound,   150
The beautiful lost swimmer, the ennuyee, the onanist, the female
    that loves unrequited, the moneymaker,
The actor and actress . . those through with their parts and those
    waiting to commence,
The affectionate boy, the husband and wife, the voter, the nominee
    that is chosen and the nominee that has failed,
The great already known, and the great anytime after to day,
The stammerer, the sick, the perfectformed, the homely,   155
The criminal that stood in the box, the judge that sat and sentenced
    him, the fluent lawyers, the jury, the audience,

The laugher and weeper, the dancer, the midnight widow, the red
  squaw,
The consumptive, the erysipalite, the idiot, he that is wronged,
The antipodes, and every one between this and them in the dark,
I swear they are averaged now . . . . one is no better than the other,   160
The night and sleep have likened them and restored them.

I swear they are all beautiful,
Every one that sleeps is beautiful . . . . every thing in the dim night
  is beautiful,
The wildest and bloodiest is over and all is peace.

Peace is always beautiful,   165
The myth of heaven indicates peace and night.

The myth of heaven indicates the soul;
The soul is always beautiful . . . . it appears more or it appears less
  . . . . it comes or lags behind,
It comes from its embowered garden and looks pleasantly on itself
  and encloses the world;
Perfect and clean the genitals previously jetting, and perfect and
  clean the womb cohering,   170
The head wellgrown and proportioned and plumb, and the bowels
  and joints proportioned and plumb.

The soul is always beautiful,
The universe is duly in order . . . . every thing is in its place,
What is arrived is in its place, and what waits is in its place;
The twisted skull waits . . . . the watery or rotten blood waits,   175
The child of the glutton or venerealee waits long, and the child of
  the drunkard waits long, and the drunkard himself waits long,
The sleepers that lived and died wait . . . . the far advanced are to
  go on in their turns, and the far behind are to go on in their
  turns,
The diverse shall be no less diverse, but they shall flow and unite
  . . . . they unite now.

[8]
The sleepers are very beautiful as they lie unclothed,
They flow hand in hand over the whole earth from east to west as
    they lie unclothed;   180
The Asiatic and African are hand in hand .. the European and
    American are hand in hand,
Learned and unlearned are hand in hand .. and male and female
    are hand in hand;
The bare arm of the girl crosses the bare breast of her lover . . . .
    they press close without lust . . . . his lips press her neck,
The father holds his grown or ungrown son in his arms with
    measureless love . . . . and the son holds the father in his arms
    with measureless love,
The white hair of the mother shines on the white wrist of the
    daughter,   185
The breath of the boy goes with the breath of the man . . . . friend
    is inarmed by friend,
The scholar kisses the teacher and the teacher kisses the scholar . . . .
    the wronged is made right,
The call of the slave is one with the master's call .. and the master
    salutes the slave,
The felon steps forth from the prison . . . . the insane becomes sane
    . . . . the suffering of sick persons is relieved,
The sweatings and fevers stop .. the throat that was unsound is
    sound .. the lungs of the consumptive are resumed .. the
    poor distressed head is free,   190
The joints of the rheumatic move as smoothly as ever, and smoother
    than ever,
Stiflings and passages open . . . . the paralysed become supple,
The swelled and convulsed and congested awake to themselves in
    condition,
They pass the invigoration of the night and the chemistry of the
    night and awake.

I too pass from the night;   195
I stay awhile away O night, but I return to you again and love you;

Why should I be afraid to trust myself to you?
I am not afraid . . . . I have been well brought forward by you;
I love the rich running day, but I do not desert her in whom I lay
    so long:
I know not how I came of you, and I know not where I go with you
    . . . . but I know I came well and shall go well.   200

I will stop only a time with the night . . . . and rise betimes.

I will duly pass the day O my mother and duly return to you;
Not you will yield forth the dawn again more surely than you will
    yield forth me again,
Not the womb yields the babe in its time more surely than I shall
    be yielded from you in my time.

LEAVES OF GRASS

[*I Sing the Body Electric*]

[1]

THE BODIES OF MEN AND WOMEN ENGIRTH ME, AND I ENGIRTH
THEM,
They will not let me off nor I them till I go with them and
respond to them and love them.

Was it dreamed whether those who corrupted their own live bodies
could conceal themselves?
And whether those who defiled the living were as bad as they who
defiled the dead?

[2]

The expression of the body of man or woman balks account,   5
The male is perfect and that of the female is perfect.

The expression of a wellmade man appears not only in his face,
It is in his limbs and joints also . . . . it is curiously in the joints of
his hips and wrists,
It is in his walk . . the carriage of his neck . . the flex of his waist and
knees . . . . dress does not hide him,
The strong sweet supple quality he has strikes through the cotton
and flannel;   10
To see him pass conveys as much as the best poem . . perhaps
more,
You linger to see his back and the back of his neck and
shoulderside.

The sprawl and fulness of babes . . . . the bosoms and heads of
    women . . . . the folds of their dress . . . . their style as we pass
    in the street . . . . the contour of their shape downwards;
The swimmer naked in the swimmingbath . . seen as he swims
    through the salt transparent greenshine, or lies on his back and
    rolls silently with the heave of the water;
Framers bare-armed framing a house . . hoisting the beams in their
    places . . or using the mallet and mortising-chisel,   15
The bending forward and backward of rowers in rowboats . . . . the
    horseman in his saddle;
Girls and mothers and housekeepers in all their exquisite offices,
The group of laborers seated at noontime with their open dinner-
    kettles, and their wives waiting,
The female soothing a child . . . . the farmer's daughter in the
    garden or cowyard,
The woodman rapidly swinging his axe in the woods . . . . the
    young fellow hoeing corn . . . . the sleighdriver guiding his six
    horses through the crowd,   20
The wrestle of wrestlers . . . . two apprentice-boys, quite grown,
    lusty, goodnatured, nativeborn, out on the vacant lot at sun-
    down after work,
The coats vests and caps thrown down . . the embrace of love and
    resistance,
The upperhold and underhold—the hair rumpled over and blinding
    the eyes;
The march of firemen in their own costumes—the play of the
    masculine muscle through cleansetting trowsers and waistbands,
The slow return from the fire . . . . the pause when the bell strikes
    suddenly again—the listening on the alert,   25
The natural perfect and varied attitudes . . . . the bent head, the
    curved neck, the counting:
Suchlike I love . . . . I loosen myself and pass freely . . . . and am at
    the mother's breast with the little child,
And swim with the swimmer, and wrestle with wrestlers, and march
    in line with the firemen, and pause and listen and count.

[3]

I knew a man . . . . he was a common farmer . . . . he was the father
    of five sons . . . . and in them were the fathers of sons . . . . and
    in them were the fathers of sons.

This man was a wonderful vigor and calmness and beauty of person;   30
The shape of his head, the richness and breadth of his manners, the
    pale yellow and white of his hair and beard, the immeasurable
    meaning of his black eyes,
These I used to go and visit him to see . . . . He was wise also,
He was six feet tall . . . . he was over eighty years old . . . . his sons
    were massive clean bearded tanfaced and handsome,
They and his daughters loved him . . . all who saw him loved him
    . . . they did not love him by allowance . . . they loved him
    with personal love;
He drank water only . . . . the blood showed like scarlet through the
    clear brown skin of his face;   35
He was a frequent gunner and fisher . . . he sailed his boat himself
    . . . he had a fine one presented to him by a shipjoiner . . . .
    he had fowling pieces, presented to him by men that loved
    him;
When he went with his five sons and many grandsons to hunt or fish
    you would pick him out as the most beautiful and vigorous of
    the gang,
You would wish long and long to be with him . . . . you would wish
    to sit by him in the boat that you and he might touch each
    other.

[4]

I have perceived that to be with those I like is enough,
To stop in company with the rest at evening is enough,   40
To be surrounded by beautiful curious breathing laughing flesh is
    enough,
To pass among them . . to touch any one . . . . to rest my arm ever
    so lightly round his or her neck for a moment . . . . what is this
    then?

I do not ask any more delight . . . . I swim in it as in a sea.

There is something in staying close to men and women and looking
    on them and in the contact and odor of them that pleases the
    soul well,
All things please the soul, but these please the soul well.   45

[5]
This is the female form,
A divine nimbus exhales from it from head to foot,
It attracts with fierce undeniable attraction,
I am drawn by its breath as if I were no more than a helpless vapor
    . . . . all falls aside but myself and it,
Books, art, religion, time . . the visible and solid earth . . the atmos-
    phere and the fringed clouds . . what was expected of heaven
    or feared of hell are now consumed,   50
Mad filaments, ungovernable shoots play out of it . . the response
    likewise ungovernable,
Hair, bosom, hips, bend of legs, negligent falling hands—all diffused
    . . . . mine too diffused,
Ebb stung by the flow, and flow stung by the ebb . . . . loveflesh
    swelling and deliciously aching,
Limitless limpid jets of love hot and enormous . . . . quivering jelly
    of love . . . . white-blow and delirious juice,
Bridegroom-night of love working surely and softly into the prostrate
    dawn,   55
Undulating into the willing and yielding day,
Lost in the cleave of the clasping and sweetfleshed day.

This is the nucleus . . . after the child is born of woman the man is
    born of woman,
This is the bath of birth . . . this is the merge of small and large and
    the outlet again.

Be not ashamed women . . your privilege encloses the rest . . it is the
    exit of the rest,   60
You are the gates of the body and you are the gates of the soul.

The female contains all qualities and tempers them . . . . she is in
     her place . . . . she moves with perfect balance,
She is all things duly veiled . . . . she is both passive and active . . . .
     she is to conceive daughters as well as sons and sons as well as
     daughters.

As I see my soul reflected in nature . . . . as I see through a mist one
     with inexpressible completeness and beauty . . . . see the bent
     head and arms folded over the breast . . . . the female I see,
I see the bearer of the great fruit which is immortality . . . . the good
     thereof is not tasted by roues, and never can be.   65

[6]

The male is not less the soul, nor more . . . . he too is in his place,
He too is all qualities . . . . he is action and power . . . . the flush of
     the known universe is in him,
Scorn becomes him well and appetite and defiance become him well,
The fiercest largest passions . . bliss that is utmost and sorrow that
     is utmost become him well . . . . pride is for him,
The fullspread pride of man is calming and excellent to the soul;   70
Knowledge becomes him . . . . he likes it always . . . . he brings
     everything to the test of himself,
Whatever the survey . . whatever the sea and the sail, he strikes
     soundings at last only here,
Where else does he strike soundings except here?

The man's body is sacred and the woman's body is sacred . . . . it is
     no matter who,
Is it a slave? Is it one of the dullfaced immigrants just landed on
     the wharf?   75

Each belongs here or anywhere just as much as the welloff . . . . just
     as much as you,
Each has his or her place in the procession.

All is a procession,
The universe is a procession with measured and beautiful motion.

Do you know so much that you call the slave or the dullfaced
    ignorant?   80
Do you suppose you have a right to a good sight . . . and he or she
    has no right to a sight?
Do you think matter has cohered together from its diffused float, and
    the soil is on the surface and water runs and vegetation sprouts
    for you . . and not for him and her?

[7]

A slave at auction!
I help the auctioneer . . . . the sloven does not half know his
    business.

Gentlemen look on this curious creature,   85
Whatever the bids of the bidders they cannot be high enough for
    him,
For him the globe lay preparing quintillions of years without one
    animal or plant,
For him the revolving cycles truly and steadily rolled.

In that head the allbaffling brain,
In it and below it the making of the attributes of heroes.   90

Examine these limbs, red black or white . . . . they are very cunning
    in tendon and nerve;
They shall be stript that you may see them.

Exquisite senses, lifelit eyes, pluck, volition,
Flakes of breastmuscle, pliant backbone and neck, flesh not flabby,
    goodsized arms and legs,
And wonders within there yet.   95

Within there runs his blood . . . . the same old blood . . the same
    red running blood;
There swells and jets his heart . . . . There all passions and desires
    . . all reachings and aspirations:

Do you think they are not there because they are not expressed in
    parlors and lecture-rooms?

This is not only one man . . . . he is the father of those who shall be
    fathers in their turns,
In him the start of populous states and rich republics,   100
Of him countless immortal lives with countless embodiments and
    enjoyments.

How do you know who shall come from the offspring of his offspring
    through the centuries?
Who might you find you have come from yourself if you could trace
    back through the centuries?

[8]
A woman at auction,
She too is not only herself . . . . she is the teeming mother of
    mothers,   105
She is the bearer of them that shall grow and be mates to the
    mothers.

Her daughters or their daughters' daughters . . who knows who shall
    mate with them?
Who knows through the centuries what heroes may come from them?

In them and of them natal love . . . . in them the divine mystery
    . . . . the same old beautiful mystery.

Have you ever loved a woman?   110
Your mother . . . . is she living? . . . . Have you been much with
    her? and has she been much with you?
Do you not see that these are exactly the same to all in all nations
    and times all over the earth?

If life and the soul are sacred the human body is sacred;
And the glory and sweet of a man is the token of manhood untainted,

And in man or woman a clean strong firmfibred body is beautiful
    as the most beautiful face.   115

Have you seen the fool that corrupted his own live body? or the
    fool that corrupted her own live body?
For they do not conceal themselves, and cannot conceal themselves.

Who degrades or defiles the living human body is cursed,
Who degrades or defiles the body of the dead is not more cursed.

LEAVES OF GRASS

[*Faces*]

[1]

Sauntering the pavement or riding the country byroads here
    then are faces,
Faces of friendship, precision, caution, sauvity, ideality,
The spiritual prescient face, the always welcome common benevolent
    face,
The face of the singing of music, the grand faces of natural lawyers
    and judges broad at the backtop,
The faces of hunters and fishers, bulged at the brows . . . . the shaved
    blanched faces of orthodox citizens,   5
The pure extravagant yearning questioning artist's face,
The welcome ugly face of some beautiful soul . . . . the handsome
    detested or despised face,
The sacred faces of infants . . . . the illuminated face of the mother
    of many children,
The face of an amour . . . . the face of veneration,
The face as of a dream . . . . the face of an immobile rock,   10
The face withdrawn of its good and bad . . a castrated face,
A wild hawk . . his wings clipped by the clipper,
A stallion that yielded at last to the thongs and knife of the gelder.

Sauntering the pavement or crossing the ceaseless ferry, here then
    are faces;
I see them and complain not and am content with all.   15

[2]

Do you suppose I could be content with all if I thought them their
    own finale?

This now is too lamentable a face for a man;
Some abject louse asking leave to be . . cringing for it,
Some milknosed maggot blessing what lets it wrig to its hole.

This face is a dog's snout sniffing for garbage;   20
Snakes nest in that mouth . . I hear the sibilant threat.

This face is a haze more chill than the arctic sea,
Its sleepy and wobbling icebergs crunch as they go.

This is a face of bitter herbs . . . . this an emetic . . . . they need no
      label,
And more of the drugshelf . . laudanum, caoutchouc, or hog's lard.   25

This face is an epilepsy advertising and doing business . . . . its
      wordless tongue gives out the unearthly cry,
Its veins down the neck distend . . . . its eyes roll till they show
      nothing but their whites,
Its teeth grit . . the palms of the hands are cut by the turned-in nails,
The man falls struggling and foaming to the ground while he
      speculates well.

This face is bitten by vermin and worms,   30
And this is some murderer's knife with a halfpulled scabbard.

This face owes to the sexton his dismalest fee,
An unceasing deathbell tolls there.

Those are really men! . . . . the bosses and tufts of the great round
      globe!

[3]
Features of my equals, would you trick me with your creased and
      cadaverous march?   35
Well then you cannot trick me.

I see your rounded never-erased flow,

I see neath the rims of your haggard and mean disguises.

Splay and twist as you like . . . . poke with the tangling fores of
    fishes or rats,
You'll be unmuzzled . . . . you certainly will.   40

I saw the face of the most smeared and slobbering idiot they had at
    the asylum,
And I knew for my consolation what they knew not;
I knew of the agents that emptied and broke my brother,
The same wait to clear the rubbish from the fallen tenement;
And I shall look again in a score or two of ages,   45
And I shall meet the real landlord perfect and unharmed, every inch
    as good as myself.

[4]
The Lord advances and yet advances:
Always the shadow in front . . . . always the reached hand bringing
    up the laggards.

Out of this face emerge banners and horses . . . . O superb! I
    see what is coming,
I see the high pioneercaps . . . . I see the staves of runners clearing
    the way,   50
I hear victorious drums.

This face is a lifeboat;
This is the face commanding and bearded . . . . it asks no odds of
    the rest;
This face is flavored fruit ready for eating;
This face of a healthy honest boy is the programme of all good.   55

These faces bear testimony slumbering or awake,
They show their descent from the Master himself.

Off the word I have spoken I except not one . . . . red white or
    black, all are deific,

In each house is the ovum . . . . it comes forth after a thousand years.

Spots or cracks at the windows do not disturb me,   60
Tall and sufficient stand behind and make signs to me;
I read the promise and patiently wait.

This is a fullgrown lily's face,
She speaks to the limber-hip'd man near the garden pickets,
Come here, she blushingly cries . . . . Come nigh to me limber-hip'd
    man and give me your finger and thumb,   65
Stand at my side till I lean as high as I can upon you,
Fill me with albescent honey . . . . bend down to me,
Rub to me with your chafing beard . . rub to my breast and
    shoulders.

[5]
The old face of the mother of many children:
Whist! I am fully content.   70

Lulled and late is the smoke of the Sabbath morning,
It hangs low over the rows of trees by the fences,
It hangs thin by the sassafras, the wildcherry and the catbrier under
    them.

I saw the rich ladies in full dress at the soiree,
I heard what the run of poets were saying so long,   75
Heard who sprang in crimson youth from the white froth and the
    water-blue.

Behold a woman!
She looks out from her quaker cap . . . . her face is clearer and more
    beautiful than the sky.

She sits in an armchair under the shaded porch of the farmhouse,
The sun just shines on her old white head.   80

Her ample gown is of creamhued linen,

Her grandsons raised the flax, and her granddaughters spun it with
    the distaff and the wheel.

The melodious character of the earth!
The finish beyond which philosophy cannot go and does not wish
    to go!
The justified mother of men!   85

[Song of the Answerer]

A YOUNG MAN CAME TO ME WITH A MESSAGE FROM HIS BROTHER,
How should the young man know the whether and when of his
    brother?
Tell him to send me the signs.

And I stood before the young man face to face, and took his right
    hand in my left hand and his left hand in my right hand,
And I answered for his brother and for men . . . . and I answered for
    the poet, and sent these signs.   5

Him all wait for . . . . him all yield up to . . . . his word is decisive
    and final,
Him they accept . . . . in him lave . . . . in him perceive themselves
    as amid light,
Him they immerse, and he immerses them.

Beautiful women, the haughtiest nations, laws, the landscape,
    people and animals,
The profound earth and its attributes, and the unquiet ocean,   10
All enjoyments and properties, and money, and whatever money
    will buy,
The best farms. . . . . others toiling and planting, and he unavoidably
    reaps,
The noblest and costliest cities . . . . others grading and building,
    and he domiciles there;
Nothing for any one but what is for him . . . . near and far are for
    him,
The ships in the offing . . . . the perpetual shows and marches on land
    are for him if they are for any body.   15

He puts things in their attitudes,
He puts today out of himself with plasticity and love,
He places his own city, times, reminiscences, parents, brothers and
 sisters, associations employment and politics, so that the rest
 never shame them afterward, nor assume to command them.

He is the answerer,
What can be answered he answers, and what cannot be answered
 he shows how it cannot be answered.   20

A man is a summons and challenge,
It is vain to skulk . . . . Do you hear that mocking and laughter?
 Do you hear the ironical echoes?

Books friendships philosophers priests action pleasure pride beat up
 and down seeking to give satisfaction;
He indicates the satisfaction, and indicates them that beat up and
 down also.

Whichever the sex . . . whatever the season or place he may go
 freshly and gently and safely by day or by night,   25
He has the passkey of hearts . . . . to him the response of the prying
 of hands on the knobs.

His welcome is universal . . . . the flow of beauty is not more
 welcome or universal than he is,
The person he favors by day or sleeps with at night is blessed.

Every existence has its idiom . . . . every thing has an idiom and
 tongue;
He resolves all tongues into his own, and bestows it upon men . .
 and any man translates . . and any man translates himself also: 30
One part does not counteract another part . . . . He is the joiner . .
 he sees how they join.

He says indifferently and alike, How are you friend? to the President
 at his levee,

And he says Good day my brother, to Cudge that hoes in the
    sugarfield;
And both understand him and know that his speech is right.

He walks with perfect ease in the capitol, 35
He walks among the Congress . . . . and one representative says to
    another, Here is our equal appearing and new.

Then the mechanics take him for a mechanic,
And the soldiers suppose him to be a captain . . . . and the sailors
    that he has followed the sea,
And the authors take him for an author . . . . and the artists for an
    artist,
And the laborers perceive he could labor with them and love them; 40
No matter what the work is, that he is one to follow it or has
    followed it,
No matter what the nation, that he might find his brothers and
    sisters there.

The English believe he comes of their English stock,
A Jew to the Jew he seems . . . . a Russ to the Russ . . . . usual and
    near . . removed from none.

Whoever he looks at in the traveler's coffeehouse claims him, 45
The Italian or Frenchman is sure, and the German is sure, and the
    Spaniard is sure . . . . and the island Cuban is sure.

The engineer, the deckhand on the great lakes or on the Mississippi
    or St. Lawrence or Sacramento or Hudson or Delaware
    claims him.

The gentleman of perfect blood acknowledges his perfect blood,
The insulter, the prostitute, the angry person, the beggar, see them-
    selves in the ways of him . . . . he strangely transmutes them,
They are not vile any more . . . . they hardly know themselves, they
    are so grown. 50

You think it would be good to be the writer of melodious verses,
Well it would be good to be the writer of melodious verses;
But what are verses beyond the flowing character you could have?
.... or beyond beautiful manners and behaviour?
Or beyond one manly or affectionate deed of an apprenticeboy?
.... or old woman? .. or man that has been in prison or is
likely to be in prison?

[Europe:
The 72d and 73d Years of These States]

SUDDENLY OUT OF ITS STALE AND DROWSY LAIR, THE LAIR OF SLAVES,
Like lightning Europe le'pt forth . . . . half startled at itself,
Its feet upon the ashes and the rags . . . . Its hands tight to the
    throats of kings.

O hope and faith! O aching close of lives! O many a sickened heart!
Turn back unto this day, and make yourselves afresh.   5

And you, paid to defile the People . . . . you liars mark:
Not for numberless agonies, murders, lusts,
For court thieving in its manifold mean forms,
Worming from his simplicity the poor man's wages;
For many a promise sworn by royal lips, and broken, and laughed at
    in the breaking,   10
Then in their power not for all these did the blows strike of personal
    revenge . . or the heads of the nobles fall;
The People scorned the ferocity of kings.

But the sweetness of mercy brewed bitter destruction, and the
    frightened rulers come back:
Each comes in state with his train . . . . hangman, priest and tax-
    gatherer . . . . soldier, lawyer, jailer and sycophant.

Yet behind all, lo, a Shape,   15
Vague as the night, draped interminably, head front and form in
    scarlet folds,
Whose face and eyes none may see,
Out of its robes only this . . . . the red robes, lifted by the arm,
One finger pointed high over the top, like the head of a snake appears.

Meanwhile corpses lie in new-made graves . . . . bloody corpses of
    young men: 20
The rope of the gibbet hangs heavily . . . . the bullets of princes are
    flying . . . . the creatures of power laugh aloud,
And all these things bear fruits . . . . and they are good.

Those corpses of young men,
Those martyrs that hang from the gibbets . . . those hearts pierced
    by the gray lead,
Cold and motionless as they seem . . live elsewhere with unslaughter'd
    vitality.   25

They live in other young men, O kings,
They live in brothers, again ready to defy you:
They were purified by death . . . . they were taught and exalted.

Not a grave of the murdered for freedom but grows seed for
    freedom . . . . in its turn to bear seed,
Which the winds carry afar and re-sow, and the rains and the
    snows nourish.   30

Not a disembodied spirit can the weapons of tyrants let loose,
But it stalks invisibly over the earth . . whispering counseling
    cautioning.

Liberty let others despair of you . . . . I never despair of you.

Is the house shut? Is the master away?
Nevertheless be ready . . . . be not weary of watching,   35
He will soon return . . . . his messengers come anon.

[*A Boston Ballad*]

CLEAR THE WAY THERE JONATHAN!
Way for the President's marshal! Way for the government cannon!
Way for the federal foot and dragoons . . . . and the phantoms
afterward.

I rose this morning early to get betimes in Boston town;
Here's a good place at the corner . . . . I must stand and see the
show.   5

I love to look on the stars and stripes . . . . I hope the fifes will play
Yankee Doodle.

How bright shine the foremost with cutlasses,
Every man holds his revolver . . . . marching stiff through Boston
town.

A fog follows . . . . antiques of the same come limping,
Some appear wooden-legged and some appear bandaged and
bloodless.   10

Why this is a show! It has called the dead out of the earth,
The old graveyards of the hills have hurried to see;
Uncountable phantoms gather by flank and rear of it,
Cocked hats of mothy mould and crutches made of mist,
Arms in slings and old men leaning on young men's shoulders.   15

What troubles you, Yankee phantoms? What is all this chattering
of bare gums?
Does the ague convulse your limbs? Do you mistake your crutches
for firelocks, and level them?

If you blind your eyes with tears you will not see the President's
    marshal,
If you groan such groans you might balk the government cannon.

For shame old maniacs! . . . . Bring down those tossed arms, and let
    your white hair be;   20
Here gape your smart grandsons . . . . their wives gaze at them from
    the windows,
See how well-dressed . . . . see how orderly they conduct themselves.

Worse and worse . . . . Can't you stand it? Are you retreating?
Is this hour with the living too dead for you?

Retreat then! Pell-mell! . . . . Back to the hills, old limpers!   25
I do not think you belong here anyhow.

But there is one thing that belongs here . . . . Shall I tell you what it
    is, gentlemen of Boston?

I will whisper it to the Mayor . . . . he shall send a committee to
    England,
They shall get a grant from the Parliament, and go with a cart to
    the royal vault.
Dig out King George's coffin . . . . unwrap him quick from the
    graveclothes . . . . box up his bones for a journey: 30
Find a swift Yankee clipper . . . . here is freight for you blackbellied
    clipper,
Up with your anchor! shake out your sails! . . . . steer straight toward
    Boston bay.

Now call the President's marshal again, and bring out the govern-
    ment cannon,
And fetch home the roarers from Congress, and make another
    procession and guard it with foot and dragoons.

Here is a centrepiece for them: 35
Look! all orderly citizens . . . . look from the windows women.

The committee open the box and set up the regal ribs and glue those
    that will not stay,
And clap the skull on top of the ribs, and clap a crown on top of the
    skull.

You have got your revenge old buster! . . . . The crown is come to
    its own and more than its own.

Stick your hands in your pockets Jonathan . . . . you are a made man
    from this day,   40
You are mighty cute . . . . and here is one of your bargains.

[*There Was a Child Went Forth*]

There was a child went forth every day,
And the first object he looked upon and received with wonder or
    pity or love or dread, that object he became,
And that object became part of him for the day or a certain part of
    the day . . . . or for many years or stretching cycles of years.

The early lilacs became part of this child,
And grass, and white and red morningglories, and white and red
    clover, and the song of the phœbe-bird,   5
And the March-born lambs, and the sow's pink-faint litter, and the
    mare's foal, and the cow's calf, and the noisy brood of the
    barnyard or by the mire of the pondside . . and the fish
    suspending themselves so curiously below there . . and the
    beautiful curious liquid . . and the water-plants with their
    graceful flat heads . . all became part of him.

And the field-sprouts of April and May became part of him . . . .
    wintergrain sprouts, and those of the light-yellow corn, and of
    the esculent roots of the garden,
And the appletrees covered with blossoms, and the fruit afterward
    . . . . and woodberries . . and the commonest weeds by the road;
And the old drunkard staggering home from the outhouse of the
    tavern whence he had lately risen,
And the schoolmistress that passed on her way to the school . . and
    the friendly boys that passed . . and the quarrelsome boys
    . . and the tidy and freshcheeked girls . . and the barefoot
    negro boy and girl,   10
And all the changes of city and country wherever he went.

His own parents . . he that had propelled the fatherstuff at night,
    and fathered him . . and she that conceived him in her womb

and birthed him . . . . they gave this child more of themselves
    than that,
They gave him afterward every day . . . . they and of them became
    part of him.

The mother at home quietly placing the dishes on the suppertable,
The mother with mild words . . . . clean her cap and gown . . . . a
    wholesome odor falling off her person and clothes as she walks by: 15
The father, strong, selfsufficient, manly, mean, angered, unjust,
The blow, the quick loud word, the tight bargain, the crafty lure,
The family usages, the language, the company, the furniture . . . .
    the yearning and swelling heart,
Affection that will not be gainsayed . . . . The sense of what is real
    . . . . the thought if after all it should prove unreal,
The doubts of daytime and the doubts of nighttime . . . the curious
    whether and how,   20
Whether that which appears so is so . . . . Or is it all flashes and specks?
Men and women crowding fast in the streets . . if they are not
    flashes and specks what are they?
The streets themselves, and the facades of houses . . . . the goods in
    the windows,
Vehicles . . teams . . the tiered wharves, and the huge crossing at
    the ferries;
The village on the highland seen from afar at sunset . . . . the river
    between,   25
Shadows . . aureola and mist . . light falling on roofs and gables
    of white or brown, three miles off,
The schooner near by sleepily dropping down the tide . . the little
    boat slacktowed astern,
The hurrying tumbling waves and quickbroken crests and slapping;
The strata of colored clouds . . . . the long bar of maroontint away
    solitary by itself . . . . the spread of purity it lies motionless in,
The horizon's edge, the flying seacrow, the fragrance of saltmarsh
    and shoremud;   30
These became part of that child who went forth every day, and who
    now goes and will always go forth every day,
And these become of him or her that peruses them now.

[*Who Learns My Lesson Complete*]

WHO LEARNS MY LESSON COMPLETE?
Boss and journeyman and apprentice? . . . . churchman and atheist?
The stupid and the wise thinker . . . . parents and offspring . . . .
    merchant and clerk and porter and customer . . . . editor,
    author, artist and schoolboy?

Draw nigh and commence,
It is no lesson . . . . it lets down the bars to a good lesson,   5
And that to another . . . . and every one to another still.

The great laws take and effuse without argument,
I am of the same style, for I am their friend,
I love them quits and quits . . . . I do not halt and make salaams.

I lie abstracted and hear beautiful tales of things and the reasons of
    things,   10
They are so beautiful I nudge myself to listen.

I cannot say to any person what I hear . . . . I cannot say it to myself
    . . . . it is very wonderful.

It is no little matter, this round and delicious globe, moving so
    exactly in its orbit forever and ever, without one jolt or the
    untruth of a single second;
I do not think it was made in six days, nor in ten thousand years,
    nor ten decillions of years,
Nor planned and built one thing after another, as an architect plans
    and builds a house.   15

I do not think seventy years is the time of a man or woman,

Nor that seventy millions of years is the time of a man or woman,
Nor that years will ever stop the existence of me or any one else.
Is it wonderful that I should be immortal? as every one is immortal,
I know it is wonderful . . . . but my eyesight is equally wonderful
    . . . . and how I was conceived in my mother's womb is equally
    wonderful,   20
And how I was not palpable once but am now . . . . and was born
    on the last day of May 1819 . . . . and passed from a babe in
    the creeping trance of three summers and three winters to
    articulate and walk . . . . are all equally wonderful.

And that I grew six feet high . . . . and that I have become a man
    thirty-six years old in 1855 . . . . and that I am here anyhow—
    are all equally wonderful;
And that my soul embraces you this hour, and we affect each other
    without ever seeing each other, and never perhaps to see each
    other, is every bit as wonderful:
And that I can think such thoughts as these is just as wonderful,
And that I can remind you, and you think them and know them to
    be true is just as wonderful,   25
And that the moon spins round the earth and on with the earth is
    equally wonderful,
And that they balance themselves with the sun and stars is equally
    wonderful.

Come I should like to hear you tell me what there is in yourself that
    is not just as wonderful,
And I should like to hear the name of anything between Sunday
    morning and Saturday night that is not just as wonderful.

[*Great Are the Myths*]

[1]

GREAT ARE THE MYTHS.... I TOO DELIGHT IN THEM,
Great are Adam and Eve .... I too look back and accept them;
Great the risen and fallen nations, and their poets, women, sages,
    inventors, rulers, warriors and priests.

Great is liberty! Great is equality! I am their follower,
Helmsmen of nations, choose your craft .... where you sail I sail,   5
Yours is the muscle of life or death .... yours is the perfect science
    .... in you I have absolute faith.

Great is today, and beautiful,
It is good to live in this age .... there never was any better.

Great are the plunges and throes and triumphs and falls of
    democracy,
Great the reformers with their lapses and screams,   10
Great the daring and venture of sailors on new explorations.

Great are yourself and myself,
We are just as good and bad as the oldest and youngest or any,
What the best and worst did we could do,
What they felt .. do not we feel it in ourselves?   15
What they wished .. do we not wish the same?

Great is youth, and equally great is old age .... great are the day
    and night;
Great is wealth and great is poverty .... great is expression and
    great is silence.

Youth large lusty and loving .... youth full of grace and force and
    fascination,

Do you know that old age may come after you with equal grace and
    force and fascination?   20

Day fullblown and splendid . . . . day of the immense sun, and action
    and ambition and laughter,
The night follows close, with millions of suns, and sleep and restoring
    darkness.

Wealth with the flush hand and fine clothes and hospitality:
But then the soul's wealth—which is candor and knowledge and
    pride and enfolding love:
Who goes for men and women showing poverty richer than wealth?   25

Expression of speech . . in what is written or said forget not that
    silence is also expressive,
That anguish as hot as the hottest and contempt as cold as the
    coldest may be without words,
That the true adoration is likewise without words and without
    kneeling.

[2]
Great is the greatest nation . . the nation of clusters of equal nations.

Great is the earth, and the way it became what it is,   30
Do you imagine it is stopped at this? . . . . and the increase
    abandoned?
Understand then that it goes as far onward from this as this is from
    the times when it lay in covering waters and gases.

Great is the quality of truth in man,
The quality of truth in man supports itself through all changes,
It is inevitably in the man . . . . He and it are in love, and never
    leave each other.   35

The truth in man is no dictum . . . . it is vital as eyesight,
If there be any soul there is truth . . . . if there be man or woman
    there is truth . . . . If there be physical or moral there is truth,

If there be equilibrium or volition there is truth . . . . if there be
    things at all upon the earth there is truth.

O truth of the earth! O truth of things! I am determined to press
    the whole way toward you,
Sound your voice! I scale mountains or dive in the sea after you.   40

[3]
Great is language . . . . it is the mightiest of the sciences,
It is the fulness and color and form and diversity of the earth . . . .
    and of men and women . . . . and of all qualities and processes;
It is greater than wealth . . . . it is greater than buildings or ships or
    religions or paintings or music.

Great is the English speech . . . . What speech is so great as the
    English?
Great is the English brood . . . . What brood has so vast a destiny as
    the English?   45
It is the mother of the brood that must rule the earth with the new
    rule,
The new rule shall rule as the soul rules, and as the love and justice
    and equality that are in the soul rule.

Great is the law . . . . Great are the old few landmarks of the law
    . . . . they are the same in all times and shall not be disturbed.
Great are marriage, commerce, newspapers, books, freetrade, rail-
    roads, steamers, international mails and telegraphs and
    exchanges.

[4]
Great is Justice;   50
Justice is not settled by legislators and laws . . . . it is in the soul,
It cannot be varied by statutes any more than love or pride or the
    attraction of gravity can,
It is immutable . . it does not depend on majorities . . . . majorities
    or what not come at last before the same passionless and exact
    tribunal.

For justice are the grand natural lawyers and perfect judges . . . . it
    is in their souls,
It is well assorted . . . . they have not studied for nothing . . . . the
    great includes the less,   55
They rule on the highest grounds . . . . they oversee all eras and
    states and administrations,

The perfect judge fears nothing . . . . he could go front to front
    before God,
Before the perfect judge all shall stand back . . . . life and death shall
    stand back . . . . heaven and hell shall stand back.

[5]
Great is goodness;
I do not know what it is any more than I know what health is . . . .
    but I know it is great.   60

Great is wickedness . . . . I find I often admire it just as much as I
    admire goodness:
Do you call that a paradox? It certainly is a paradox.

The eternal equilibrium of things is great, and the eternal overthrow
    of things is great,
And there is another paradox.

Great is life . . and real and mystical . . wherever and whoever,   65
Great is death . . . . Sure as life holds all parts together, death holds
    all parts together;
Sure as the stars return again after they merge in the light, death is
    great as life.